Words To Lift Your Spirits

Dale Brown

Author's Note

I have always believed that motivation is a gift to be shared with everyone. Over the years I have read literally hundreds of books, and articles on the subject. From the father of the positive thinking movement, Norman Vincent Peale, to little known authors yet to be recognized, I have come to the conclusion that motivation is an art that breeds a familiarity in every message – a constant reinforcement to our own philosophy.

This book is a collection of thoughts and anecdotes that I have collected over the years. It is my hope that it too will reinforce your own positive thinking philosophy.

Dale Brown

I apologize for any author that I did not know and did not give credit to.

D A L E ▲ B R O W N ▲ E N T E R P R I S E S , ▲ I N C .

2354 S. Acadian Thruway • Suite E • Baton Rouge, LA 70808

Phone (225) 387-2233 • **FAX** (225) 387-2263

WORDS TO LIFT YOUR SPIRITS

Table of Contents

Always a Solution

by Dale Brown

Each one of us roams the earth with our own special uniqueness. We are all different – we all have a distinctive being for who we are, what we see and feel, and how we handle it. Yet, there are two common factors that we each possess. The first factor that can be said about all of us is that we will constantly be facing adversity. There will always be struggles to overcome. Hurdles must be cleared by everyone that lives. The second factor is that we each have the ability to respond in any way that we fashion.

Steven Covey, the renowned author, breaks the word responsibility into two words: "respond–ability." He believes firmly in the second factor by saying we have the **ABILITY** to **RESPOND** to any given circumstance in any manner we desire. What it comes down to (and what life always comes down to) is ATTITUDE! It takes training and the development of habits to find a positive attitude about adverse situations, but we are all capable of reaching that plateau.

The attitude must be that a problem is actually a test. I once read from a great political leader, that true leaders are not discovered until tough times arise. Winston Churchill was an extremely obscure leader until World War II nearly destroyed his country. It was his fearless attitude and leadership during a bleak and troubled time that people actually discovered what kind of man he was.

An ancient Chinese proverb tells us that "Wild times create heroes". It is absolutely true. General George S. Patton was silently worried that World War II was going to end before he was able to establish his place in history. Now certainly wishing for war to continue is unreasonable, but you can get the idea in comparison to those who were scared of going to battle.

Want to turn a disaster into a monumental success? Think back to the scientist at 3M's laboratories that was working on a superior glue to be used in a new product. The problem was, that all of his work backfired. The glue just barely held. But hey, *"wild times create heroes"*. This scientist, instead of pouting or getting angry, put on his thinking cap to try and discover a use for this new, very weak adhesive. Soon on the market from 3M were *"Post-it-Note pads."* Everyone in the world uses them. They have made millions for 3M.

There is always a solution. It just sometimes takes brave souls to search for them! So, the next time you come across *"troubled waters"*, don't be afraid to drop your line in there. You might be surprised at the results!!

Positive Attitude

by Dale Brown

So much of life comes from our views and beliefs and I can't imagine living life to its fullest without a positive attitude. The best part of our attitude is that we decide what type of attitude we want to display. This is so difficult for many to believe, but if you have a bad attitude, it is because you choose to have one. People are not born with positive mental attitudes. Somewhere down the road, at some point in your life, for whatever reason, they chose to look at the positive side of all of the circumstances surrounding their life. That doesn't mean that they don't have a bad day or that they never get angry or depressed. Those are all human emotions that each and every one of us must deal with the negative in a much different manner than if you have a poor attitude. A poor attitude will throw gas on the fire of negative happenings. A good attitude will throw water on that same fire and put it out.

Something to remember to cultivate a positive attitude is to always be full of enthusiasm. Enthusiasm and positive attitudes feed off of each other. If you are enthusiastic, you will look at things in a positive light. If you have a positive attitude, you will find enthusiasm much quicker. I don't think I have ever met a person with a positive attitude that wasn't beaming full of overwhelming enthusiasm. These kind of people are contagious. They spread this exciting feeling to those around them and soon there is an epidemic started. A positive epidemic!

Speaking under these terms, if you are cultivating a positive attitude, stay away from those who have bad attitudes. Winners surround themselves with winners. Oil and water don't mix, and neither do good and bad attitudes. Never cease trying to help those with poor attitudes on life, but don't let them pull you down in the process.

Just because you have a positive attitude, don't think bad things aren't going to happen to you– They are! A positive mental attitude is not about what happens to you, but how you view those happenings. There are no such things as problems, only opportunities. Adversity is not a bad thing, but actually a test to prove the greatness of your human spirit.

Finally, unless you have experienced the long-range effects of a positive mental attitude, you can't begin to believe the mental and physical energy it will give. There is nothing greater in the world than waking up in the morning enthused and excited about another day.

Always Try to Do Your Best.
Never Give Up and God will Take Care of Everything Else!

ONE DAY AT A TIME

There are two days in every week
that should be free from worry and anxiety.

*T*here are two days in every week about which we should not worry, two days which should be kept free from fear and apprehension.

*O*ne of these days is YESTERDAY, with it's mistakes and cares, it's faults and blunders, it's aches and pains. Yesterday has passed forever beyond our control. All the money in the world cannot bring back yesterday. We cannot undo a single act we performed; we cannot erase a single word Said – YESTERDAY IS GONE!

*T*he other day we should not worry about is TOMORROW with Its possible burdens, it's large promise and poor performance. Tomorrow is also beyond our immediate control. Tomorrow's sun will rise, either in splendor or behind a mask of clouds – but it will rise. Until it does we have no stake in tomorrow, for it is yet unborn.

*T*his leaves only one day – TODAY! Any man can fight the battle of just one day. It is only when you and I have the burdens in those two awful eternities – YESTERDAY and TOMORROW – that we break down.

The Young Man and the Starfish

Vision without action is merely a dream.
Action without vision just passes the time.
Vision with action can change the world.
—*Joel Arthur Barker*

A wise man was taking a sunrise walk along the beach. In the distance he caught sight of a young man who seemed to be dancing along the waves. As he got closer he saw that the young man was picking up starfish from the sand and tossing them gently into the ocean. "What are you doing?" the wise man asked.
"The sun is coming up and the tide is going out; if I don't throw them in they'll die."
"But young man, there are miles and miles of beach with starfish all along it – you can't possibly make a difference."
The young man bent down, picked up another starfish, and threw it lovingly back into the ocean, past the breaking waves. "It made a difference for that one", he replied.

(A Story Inspired By Loren Eisley)

PERSISTENCE

Persistence is the key that unlocks the door to success.

In the quest for success everyone must encounter the closed door marked failure. And, most people will stop dead in their tracks because they don't think they have the key to open it. But, what they don't realize it is merely an obstacle they can unlock with the key of persistence.

People who are successful never quit because their persistence won't let them. They realize that failure is merely a detour to their goal or challenge. Oh, they hear it can't be done, but they don't listen because they keep their eyes focused on the goal. They don't let failure distract them.

Getting knocked down is no disgrace: staying there is. Look at the history of defeats suffered by one of the greatest men of all times; yet he had the courage to persist:

- In 1832 he lost his job and was defeated for the legislature.
- In 1833 he failed in business.
- In 1835 his sweetheart died.
- In 1836 he had a nervous breakdown.
- In 1838 he was defeated for Speaker.
- In 1854 he was defeated for Senate.
- In 1856 he was defeated for nomination for Vice-President.
- In 1858 he was again defeated for the Senate.

But, in 1860 Abraham Lincoln was elected President of the United States. He knew the greatest principle of success was that if he persisted long enough he would win. Persistence is the key that unlocks the door to success.

THE SNAKE
That Poisons Everybody

IT TOPPLES GOVERNMENTS, WRECKS MARRIAGES, RUINS CAREERS, BUSTS REPUTATIONS, CAUSES HEARTACHES, NIGHTMARES, INDIGESTIONS, SPAWNS SUSPICION, GENERATES GRIEF, DISPATCHES INNOCENT PEOPLE TO CRY IN THEIR PILLOWS. EVEN IT'S NAME HISSES. IT'S CALLED GOSSIP. OFFICE GOSSIP, SHOP GOSSIP, PARTY GOSSIP. IT MAKES HEADLINES AND HEADACHES. BEFORE YOU REPEAT A STORY, ASK YOURSELF: IS IT TRUE? IS IS FAIR? IS IT NECESSARY? IF NOT, SHUT UP.

A message as published in the Wall Street Journal by United Technologies Corporation, Hartford, Connecticut 06101

With the beginning of a New Year many of us vow our New Year's resolutions only to forget them by Easter. But, for those who have the best of intentions or for those who have yet to get around to it, here is a simple resolution to refer to throughout the year

◆ No one will get out of this world alive. Resolve therefore in the year to maintain a sense of values.

◆ Take care of yourself. Good health is everyone's major source of wealth. Without it, happiness is almost impossible.

◆ Resolve to be cheerful and helpful. Avoid zealots. They are generally humorless.

◆ Resolve to listen more and talk less. No one ever learns anything by talking. Be leery of advice. Wise men don't need it, and fools won't heed it.

◆ Resolve to be tender with the young, compassionate with the aged, sympathetic with the striving and tolerant of the weak and the wrong. Sometimes in life you will have been all of these.

◆ Do not equate money with success. There are many successful money-makers who are miserable failures as human beings. What counts most about success is how a man achieves it.

◆ People will be unreasonable, illogical and self centered. Love them anyway.

◆ If you do good, people will accuse you of selfish motives. Do good anyway.

◆ The good you do will be forgotten tomorrow. Do it anyway.

◆ And finally, resolve to love, next year, someone you didn't love this year. Because Love is the most enriching ingredient of life.

BUILD ME A SON

During the early days of World War II in the Pacific, General Douglas McArthur wrote this simple prayer to his son in the Philippines.

Build me a son O' Lord, who will be strong enough to know he is weak, and brave enough to face himself when he is afraid; one who will be proud and unbending in honest defeat and humble and gentle in victory.

Build me a son whose wishes will not take the place of deeds; a son who will know how Thee– and that to know himself is the foundation stone of knowledge.

Lead him, I pray, not in the path of ease and comfort, but under the stress and spur of difficulties and challenge. Here let him learn to stand up in the storm; here let him learn compassion for those who fail.

Build me a son whose heart will be clear, whose goal will be high, a son who will master himself before he seeks to master other men, one who will reach into the future, yet never forget the past.

And after all these things are his, add, I pray, enough of a sense of humor, so that he may always be serious, yet never take himself too seriously. Give him humility, so that he may always remember the simplicity of true greatness, the open mind of true wisdom, and the meekness of true strength.

Then, I his father, will dare to whisper, "I have not lived in vain".

THE COLD WITHIN

Six humans were trapped by
happenstance in black and bitter
cold, each one possessed a stick of
wood or so the stories told.

In their dying fire in need of logs,
the first man held his stick back
because on the faces around the fire
he noticed one was black.

The next man looking across the
way saw one not of his church and
couldn't bring himself to give his
stick of birch.

The third man sat in tattered
clothes, he gave his coat a hitch,
why should his log be put to use to
warm the idle rich.

The rich man sat back and thought
of the wealth he had in store and
how to keep what he had earned
from those lazy shiftless poor.

The black man's face bespoke
revenge as the fire passed from
sight for all he could see in his stick
of wood was a chance to spite the
white.

And the last man of this forlorn
group did not accept for gain giving
only to those who gave was the
way he played the game.

Their logs held tight in death's still
hands was proof of human sin, they
didn't die from the cold without,
they died from the cold within.

Until we all overcome our own
prejudices and work together to
solve our problems, the problem is
only going to get worse.

Jay Patrick Kinney

Prescription for Life

To laugh often and love much; To win the respect of intelligent
persons and the affection of children; to earn the approval of
honest critics and endure the betrayal of false friends; To
appreciate beauty; To find the best in others; To give of one's self
without the slightest thought of return; to have accomplished a
task, whether by a healthy child, a rescued soul, a garden patch
or a redeemed social condition; To have played and laughed with
enthusiasm and sung with exultation; To know that even one life
has breathed easier because you have lived; This is to have
succeeded!

Henry David Thoreau

WAKE UP THE GIANT

"The one thing that will guarantee the successful conclusion of a doubtful undertaking is the faith in the beginning that we can do it".
William James

Do you have the courage to wake the sleeping giant?

There isn't a ruler, a yardstick or a measuring tape in the entire world large enough to compute the strength and capabilities of the giant who is fast asleep within you. Its size and power are unlimited. It's force is that of a million dynamos. It's tireless energy is beyond all comprehension.

It's the giant of your untapped potential; your latent ability to unfold, to develop, and to grow... but it will continue to lie there peacefully asleep until you decide to wake it up.

Like the desert lacking water, too often people endure shortages In their lives, when all they have to do is simply open the valves, the valves of SUCCESS ATTITUDES, SUCCESS HABITS, and a PLAN OF ACTION to achieve them.

The giant who sleeps within all of us will come alive only in direct proportion to the personal belief and conviction we hold. Those who utilize the full power and capacity of their inner giant aren't motivated by a government, a corporation, or society. They wake up the giant by taking firm control of their abilities, talent, and skills. They tap their potential by taking action in a personal way.

FAITH, BELIEF, AND CONVICTION are the keys, the spurs, and loud alarm that will wake up the sleeping giant within all of us.

The Price of $UCCE$$

Are you willing to pay the price for success?

What brings one man success in life, and what is it that brings mediocrity or failure to others? In short, some men expect to pay the price of success, and the others, tho they may claim ambition and a desire to succeed, are unwilling to pay the price.

So what then is that price of success? Simply, it is determination, sacrifice, and persistence. You see, sacrifice is the choice to take the road less traveled, full of its bumps, turns and road blocks. Persistence is the will that drives a person to endure that sometimes bumpy ride.

All too often failure blinds men to the success that lies just behind the next bend in the road. It is only those with the determination and the will to win who realize that nothing has ever been accomplished without first encountering failure Those who continually persist, overcome those obstacles and ultimately achieve excellence. Sure it is difficult to sacrifice and persist. But that's why so many men are content to wallow in mediocrity. They remain on the beaten paths because they are the beaten men. They accept the uneasy and inadequate contentment that comes with mediocrity.

It is only those who are willing to endure the pain of the struggle that will ultimately enjoy the rewards of success.

Are you willing to pay the price?

WE MAKES ME STRONGER

Geese don't get the big press coverage like sea gulls. Most think them unattractive. They are ordinary birds that migrate twice a year.

Like the blue angels, they fly wing tip to wing tip and you can actually hear the beat of their wings whistling through the air in unison.

And "unison" is the key word with geese because that's the secret of the birds strength. Together, cooperating as a flock, geese can fly a 70% longer range. The leader of the group cuts a path through the air resistance which creates a helping uplift for the two birds behind them. In turn, their beating makes it easier on the birds behind them.

Each bird takes his turn at being the leader. The tired ones fan out to the edge of the V for a breather and the rested ones surge toward the front of the V to drive the flock onward.

If a goose becomes too exhausted and has to drop out of the flock, he is never abandoned. A stronger member of the flock will follow the failing, weak one to his resting place or wait until he's well enough to fly again.

Yes, the geese rarely get a lot of TV time or find themselves the subject of the artist, but they are indeed a great species of bird and definitely a role model for all to learn from.

WE does make **ME** stronger.

Believe In Yourself
Anything is possible for those who believe.

Belief begins with belief in yourself. In the mirror you're looking at your best friend or your worst enemy. Your world revolves around you. It starts and ends in your heart. What you are and hope to be begins with belief in yourself.

You believed you could walk when you took your first step. You believed you could talk when you said your first word. You believed you could learn when you started school. You believed you could succeed and you probably did because you believed; or you failed because you didn't believe.

Some of our most brilliant contributors to our heritage faced repeated criticisms from others. Take for instance the Spanish painter, Pablo Picasso. He could barely read or write at the age of 10 and he was considered a hopeless pupil.

Or Albert Einstein, whose poor performance in school prompted a teacher to ask him to drop out, telling him he would never amount to anything.

Each of these people didn't give up because they didn't give up on themselves. Their life was a product of their own thoughts not the opinions or thoughts of others.

You see your whole life is based on belief-faith of one kind or another.

By believing in yourself, you have the ability to attain whatever you seek. Within you is every potential you can imagine. Always aim higher than you believe you can reach. The only real limitations you will encounter are those which you place on our own mind. So, often you'll discover that when your talents are set free by your imagination, you can achieve any goal.

The difference between a winner and a loser is just a matter of time

LAZY FAILURE

It is amazing how winner's and loser's perception of time differ.

Why is it that winners never have enough time, while losers always seem to have too much? The answer is simple, failures just don't work very hard. Oh they will tell you how hard they work and how much they do. But, the sad fact is they do very little.

Have you ever heard a winner talk about how much they have accomplished? Rarely, they are so busy that they don't have time and they really aren't concerned what others might think. On the other hand, losers are so busy coming up with excuses as to why they can't do something, they never accomplish anything.

Losers are easily distracted because they are clock watchers. Five o'clock strikes and like Cinderella they are out the door.

You see, losers don't really enjoy their jobs. In fact, when you ask them when was the last time they got a reward from their job, they probably said, "When the electricity went out and we went home early."

Winners enjoy their jobs because they have found a vocation they love. People who enjoy their work— work harder. Their reward is in the satisfaction of doing their job well.

So, what then, is the main difference between winners and losers? The answer is simple— losers are just plain lazy.

Have you checked your clock lately?

There are three basic personality types when it comes to time management

Manage Your Time

There are those people who spend all their time planning and making lists. They are so busy improving their lists and updating their plans that they never seem to achieve their goals.

Then there are those who are so busy doing, that they never have time to access the value of how they are spending their time, and as a result they never really enjoy it.

And finally, there are those who don't value their time. They take for granted that there will always be tomorrow to make plans and accomplish goals. But what they don't realize is they will run out of time before they have the time do it!

None of these perceptions of time are healthy or necessary. You see, God intends that we enjoy our lives. That includes our work, our families, our friends, and our play.

How then do we manage our time more effectively?

First, we must set priorities. What needs to come first in our life? Family will probably be at the top of most people's list, but all too often the family gets pushed to the rear because we let the pressures of the outside world interfere with our good intentions.

Setting priorities is only the first step, but sticking to the commitment is the hardest. It takes self discipline, but a wise investment of time is a wise investment in life. Without planning and priorities, our lives can slip away quickly. The way we invest our time determines our happiness and success because our time is our life. We can either spend it foolishly or fruitlessly, or we can invest it wisely.

Set priorities and stick with your commitment.

DALE BROWN

Your thought pattern will determine your life pattern.

We have all heard the old adage, "You are what you think". But, believe it or not, your thought condition will influence your life condition.

Many of us hurt our chance for success by sabotaging ourselves with negative thought patterns. And, it is those negative thought patterns that will ultimately influence our behavior. Are you one of those people who expect failure? Too often people program themselves that they are going to fail before they even begin to try. They lack the self-esteem because they don't think they deserve success. But, the truth is everyone deserves success. And, it is in everyone's grasp if they would adjust their thought condition from I can't to I can.

Negative Thought Condition

The second influence to your thought condition is the people surrounding you. Negative thinkers tend to surround themselves with negative and discouraging people. They feel comfortable in these surroundings because they don't have to live up to anyone's expectations. And, therefore, they have an excuse to fail. These people are dangerous because their views are very contagious and erode self esteem.

Do you surround yourself with people who believe in you, lift you, and help you feel good about yourself? Or do you spend time with people who bring you down?

If the world around you is negative, chances are you are too. On the other hand, if you surround yourself with positive, uplifting thoughts, you'll notice an almost immediate rise in your spirits.

Positive results begin with a positive thought condition.

LIVING IN THE PRESENT

I believe that only one person in a thousand knows the trick of really living in the present.

Most of us spend 59 minutes an hour living in the past, with regret for lost joys, or shame for things badly done — or in a future which we either long for or dread.

Yet the past is gone beyond prayer, and

A miracle happens each day, but we often fail to notice.

every minute you spend in the vain effort to anticipate the future is a moment lost.

There is only one world, the world pressing against you at this minute.

There is only one minute in which you are alive, this minute— here and now. The only way to live is by accepting each minute as an unrepeatable miracle.

Which is exactly what it is— a miracle and unrepeatable!

So, don't run through life so fast that you forget not only where you have been, but also where you are going. Life is not a race, but a journey to be savored each step of the way.

Storm Jameson

EXCUSES

Excuses are tools with which persons with n[o] purpose in view build for themselves gre[at] monuments of nothin[g]

Take for instance theses excuses:

I'm Not Worthy • I'm not Smart Enough • I Feel Inferior • I'm Black • I'm a Woman I'm Jewish • I'm Poor • I'm Too Old • I'm Too Young • I'll Fail

You see, these excuses are used in order to avoid failure. but how can we succeed without first failing? You have to learn from your failures and build success on them.

First realize that you are worthy of success by believing in your abilities. Don't use excuses. Do you think that these people use the excuse of age to accomplish their dreams?

• Mickey Mantle, at age 20, hit 23 home runs in his first full year in the major leagues.

• Gold Meir was 71 when she became Prime Minister of Israel

• George Bernard Shaw was 94 when one of his plays was produced.

• Mozart was just seven when his first composition was published.

These people have proven that you're never too young or too old to fulfill your dreams. They recognized that the excuse of age had little to do with ability to achieve success. Don't use excuses as a means to procrastination. The longer you wait the more elusive the goal becomes. Start now. Yes you may fail, but it is how you respond to failure that will ultimately determine your success.

It's up to you!

Ten Causes Of FAILURE

What lies behind you and what lies ahead is of little importance when compared to what lies within you.

Oliver Wendell Holmes

Most people don't view failure as an opportunity to evaluate themselves. They refuse to take responsibility for their failure and will pass it off as their fate. However, what they don't realize is that without self examination, they just may make the same mistake again. They will never understand that failure is the very foundation upon that which success is built. Therefore, when you fail, ask yourself these ten simple questions. Chances are you will find your answer.

1. Did I have a definite purpose or goal?

2. Did I have the proper amount of ambition to move past mediocrity?

3. Did I have the proper mental attitude?

4. Did I lack self-discipline?

5. Did I lack vision and imagination to recognize favorable opportunities?

6. Did I use excuses such as race, sex, or circumstances as a reason to quit?

7. Did I have the proper amount of faith?

8. Did I have enough mental toughness?

9. Did I lack proper work ethic?

10. Did I lack the persistence to carry a task through to the end?

You can only understand success by first understanding failure. It is the driving force that propels us to greatness.

Do you get caught up in the anticipation of the future or do you live in the eternity of the past?

Do you get caught up in the anticipation of the future or do you live in the eternity of the past?

Today is in the full bloom of life. The petals of yesterday have shriveled into the past and tomorrow is an unopened bud, a bud that may be blackened by the frosts of fate. And the future is but a seed not yet planted - of unknown quantity.

But today - today is a gorgeous blossom of beauty and fragrance. It is yours - for today.

Today is a new page in the book of life. Upon it, and upon It only, can you write a record for your accomplishments. It awaits your pen, but once turned, it is gone forever. Yesterday is a page turned. You cannot add one line to it, nor erase one word from it, it is closed forever and can affect the new page only as it has affected your heart and your courage. Your mistakes and fears of yesterday need not be carried forward in the ledger of life. The past holds no mortgage on today. Today is a loaded gun - yesterday a spent bullet. Tomorrow is your target. On it will be recorded your aim of today. Yesterday is gone, tomorrow unknown. But today - today is yours, an unmeasurable treasure house of golden opportunities, a sea of unfathomed possibilities, a forest of budding prospects.

Today is the first clear note in your song of life. It is the color tube from which you will pattern your future.

There are fourteen good working hours in today- and ten hours for thought and rest; No man has yet discovered the limit of accomplishments that may be crowded into them.

The only true limits to your potential is your imagination.

In each of us lies the unlimited potential of greatness. The only thing that will hold you back from realizing your dreams is yourself. Therefore, the first step to overcoming this great hurdle is to begin believing in yourself.

Don't underestimate your self worth by comparing yourself to others. It is because we are each different, that each of us is very special. Each of us has some sort of special talent. Don't be afraid to use it. Your dreams will always be dreams unless you begin now.

To paraphrase Edmund O'Neill, "Always aim higher than you believe you can reach. So often, you'll discover that when your talents are set free by your imagination, you can achieve any goal."

UNLIMITED POTENTIAL

If people offer you their help or wisdom as you go through life, accept it gratefully. You can learn much from those who have gone before you. But, never be afraid or hesitant to step off the accepted path and strike off on your own, if your heart tells you it's right.

Always believe you will ultimately succeed at whatever you do.

Regard failure as a perfect opportunity to show yourself how strong you truly are.

Believe in persistence, discipline, and above all, always believe in yourself. You are meant to be whatever you dream of becoming".

Dare to Dream - *the only true limits to your potential is your imagination.*

Whose Job Is It?

It's amazing what can be accomplished when no one cares who gets the credit.

There once was a story about four people named Everybody, Somebody, Anybody and Nobody. There was an important job to be done and Everybody was asked to do it. Everybody was sure Somebody would do it. but Nobody did it. Somebody got angry about that, because it was Everybody's job. Everybody thought Anybody could do it but Nobody realized that everybody won't do it. It

ended up that everybody blamed Somebody when Nobody did what Anybody could have done.

In today's competitive world, people are

always trying to gain the upper edge. But, all too often people either take the task upon themselves or they expect that someone else will take care of the job for them. And, in the end the job never seems to get finished or it is never successful because it lacked that winning ingredient called **teamwork**. If only that person who took that job on by himself had asked the person standing by to help- in the end everyone

COURAGE

The sign of a great leader is his courage to stand alone for the ideal, but together with his people in victory.

Vince Lombard once said. **"Leaders are made. they are not born".**

If that is true, what then makes a great leader? Oh, I suppose you could look back in history and find numerous examples of great leadership, but there would probably be one characteristic that would resurface time and time again. That characteristic - Courage.

A great leader will take an idea that inspires hope in people, and lead them to change with a little regard for himself. Courage begins with that ideal to speak out alone, but ends standing together with his people in victory.

Robert Kennedy once described leadership as -"Each time a man stands up for any idea, or acts to improve the lot of others, or strikes out against injustice, he sends forth a tiny ripple of hope, and crossing each other from a million different centers of energy and daring, those ripples build a current that can sweep down the mightiest wall of oppression and resistance.

Few are willing to brave the disapproval of their fellows, the censure of their colleagues, the wrath of their society. Moral courage is a rarer commodity than bravery in battle or great intelligence. Yet it is the one essential, vital quality for those who seek to change a world that yields most painfully to change."

The role of most leaders is to get the people to think more of the leader, but the role of the exceptional leader is to get people to think more of themselves.

DALE BROWN

SO SIMPLE
Alvin F. "Doggie" Julian

Little Johnny came home one night and started bombing his Dad with questions. This particular night his Dad was tired and wanted to put on his slippers and rest. But little Johnny persisted. Finally, his dad went over to the bookcase and got a map of the world. He tore the map into small pieces, got some scotch tape, and said, "Here, Johnny! Take this map of the world and put it together. When you are finished I will answer all the questions you want".

The father thought it would keep him busy for a couple of hours but, to his amazement, Johnny was back in twenty minutes with the map of the world put together perfectly. Every country and continent was right where it belonged. The father .said, "Why Johnny, how did you do it?" Shaking his head in amazement, "Why, son, I should be asking you questions!"

Little Johnny smiled and replied, "It was easy, Dad. Look!" He held the map up to his father and then turned it slowly to the other side revealing a simplistic picture of a young boy. "You see Dad, if you put that boy together right, the world will be alright."

THE DANGEROUS PEOPLE

"No one so thoroughly appreciates the value of constructive criticism as the one who is giving it" **Hal Chadwick**

The dangerous people are not the ones who hit you with clubs and rob you with guns!
The thief won't attack your character traits or belittle your abilities to your face.
It likely will be a well meaning friend, who merely crushes your will to win!
No, he doesn't rob you at the point of a gun. He simply says, "It can't be done"!
When pointing to thousands who already are, he smiles and says,
"Oh they're superior, by far, Personality, wise, and ability too.
They're way ahead of what others can do!"
It matters not that his words are untrue, for you feel others must surely know you.
So, you're robbed of your dreams, your hopes to succeed;
robbed of material blessing received;
Robbed of your faith that says, "I can",
And robbed by an ignorant gunless friend!
So, the deadliest of me is not "he with a gun",
But the one who tells you, "It can't be done".
For that taken by burglars can be gotten again; But who can replace
YOUR WILL TO WIN?

Dreams

The difference between a realist and dreamer is–
A realist sees the chance for failure and the
dreamer sees the chance for success.
Dale Brown

There comes a time, a time in every man's life when he is faced with a personal crisis or monumental challenge. It is at this time, that a man discovers what truly exists deep down inside his soul.

Great men have dreams, hopes and aspirations, average men do not. It is the strength of the will, and the fire of determination blazing inside the soul that leads men to fulfill these dreams, hopes and aspirations.

Great men reach deep down inside their soul to accept, fight and conquer any and all challenges. Average men never reach this deep and therefore falter and are defeated. Your will, and the amount of intensity and determination with which you meet challenges, has no correlation with size, speed or ability.

Along the path of life, in search of our dreams, hopes and aspirations, there are many obstacles, many challenges, many battles. Great men are willing to pay the price for success and victory. Average men are not, and later live to regret it.

You see, the will is the backbone of the soul. The fire within great men's souls blaze greater, and their will is strengthened with each battle, each victory. These men continually strive to reach their ultimate goal – their dreams.

Robert Kennedy once said. "Some men dream things as they are and ask WHY? I have dreams that never were and say WHY NOT?"

WHAT IS *Fame?*

Few were more familiar with success and fame than the legendary Babe Ruth. But for all its worth, his success never really afforded him what he really needed.

Babe Ruth once wrote, "Fame is a spotlight one minute and bull's-eye the next. The people who cheer loudest when you succeed are those who throw pop bottles the hardest when you fail.

It's all very well to be known all over the world. It pays big dividends. But dividends alone won't make a man happy. I think it is better to be known well by a few good friends - trusted and liked and respected by them in spite of all of one's weaknesses and shortcomings - than to be cheered on every continent by people who think you're great.

Most of the people who have really counted in my life were not famous. Nobody ever heard of them— except those who knew and loved them. I have written my name on thousands and thousands of baseballs in my life. But I knew an old priest once who wrote his name on but just a few simple hearts. How I envy him! He was not trying to please a crowd. He was merely trying to please his own immortal soul. So fame never came to him.

I am listed as a famous home-runner, yet beside that obscure priest, who was good and wise, I never got to first base".

You see, success isn't measured in home runs or fame, it is measured by men's kindness towards other men.

MOTIVATION

MANAGER

"Motivation is the art of getting people to do what you want them to do because they want to do it"
Dwight Eisenhower

The biggest motivation problem managers have is getting the people excited about their jobs for a long period of time.

Some guys are great ball players in that they can run and jump and shoot. The same is true in the world of business. They can be great in their jobs, but if you want motivated people - those who can get excited about their jobs, then look to those who hustle, who are loyal, who persevere. They're your key people. Those things are a real talent and should be recognized and appreciated.

I used to think that you could motivate anyone, but I don't believe that anymore. What you can do is maybe motivate them for 48 hours, but all you can really do in the long run is help them to discover something within themselves, help them turn that switch on. You can he patient. You can be encouraging. But true motivation has got to come from within themselves.

How then do you bring that best out? First, good managers must understand the real role of leadership. Too often people in roles of management get caught up in positions of power and their egos carry them away. As a result, the employee begins to resent the leader and is then less likely to be motivated or loyal.

Exceptional leaders know that their role is to get their employees to start thinking more of themselves. It is the simple principle of self worth. The more self worth an employee has, the more valuable they become to the company.

You see, if they feel good about themselves and their abilities, the more productive and more motivated they become. It is only then a person will reach down within himself to discover his greatest potential.

Dale Brown

To Succeed One Must FAIL.

Willie Stargell is known as one of the greatest sports heroes. His success includes two World Series and the National League's Most Valuable Player. He has lived the American dream. So what then was his prescription for success?

He once said, "To succeed, one must fail; and the more you fail, the more you learn about succeeding. The person who has never tried and failed will never succeed.

The key to surviving a failure is to bend, not break. At times, I bent like a palm tree in a hurricane, but I never broke. One must be flexible to learn from failure. Knowledge always takes the edge off fear. Baseball exposed me to my two biggest foes, pride and judgement, and gave me a system to handle both.

You don't survive long on pride. For pride makes you spend too much time gloating on your success or worrying about your failure to learn. Pride is a dangerous ingredient for anyone who has his sights set on a dream. It inhibits your flexibility, stops you from gaining the knowledge you need. It also stops you from learning from your best teacher, your failures.

Judgement is equally dangerous. Each person has different abilities and goals, Judgement traps you within your comparisons to others instead of allowing you the freedom of your own dream. Worry about your own results. To be successful, one must abandon both pride and judgement or be doomed to mediocrity forever.

So find a dream and never give up on it. And never forget the value of touching, feeling and living every portion of life that comes your way. There's a lot to be learned in living every day."

DALE BROWN

ENCOURAGEMENT

Encouragement is the seed of inspiration.

In the early nineteenth century, a young man in London aspired to be a writer. But everything seemed to be against him. He had never been able to attend school more than four years. His father had been thrown in jail, and he often knew the pangs of hunger. He found a job in a rat infested warehouse, and he slept in the dismal slums of London. He had so little confidence in his writing abilities that he sneaked out and mailed his first manuscript in the dead of the night so nobody would laugh at him. Story after story was refused. Until one day, one was finally accepted. True, he wasn't paid a shilling for it, but one editor had praised him. One editor had given him recognition.

Because of the praise, recognition, and encouragement of just one person, this young boy began to transform into one of our most noted writers of all time. His name - Charles Dickens.

You see, by telling your child, spouse, or employee that he or she is stupid, has no gift for a certain task, or is doing it all wrong, you have destroyed almost every incentive to try to improve. Use the opposite technique - be liberal with encouragement, make the task seem easy to do. Let the person know that you have faith in his or her abilities, and that they have an undeveloped flair for the task - you will be amazed what he or she is capable of accomplishing with just a little encouragement.

Psychologist Jess Lair once said, "Praise is like sunlight to the warm human spirit; we cannot flower and grow without it. And yet, while most of us are only too ready to apply to others the cold wind of criticism, we are somehow reluctant to give our fellow man the warm sunshine of praise".

Portrait of a Friend

A faithful friend is the medicine of life.
Ecclesiasticus

His love for you is tops when you're at the bottom.
He looks you up when the rest of the world looks down on you.
He lets you step on his toes to help you get on your feet.
He shows you the meaning of friendship—not the meanness of it.
He shoots straight with you— not at you.
He knows most of your faults—and cares least.
When you're wrong he tells it to you— not the rest of the world.
He doesn't complain when you neglect him— but beefs when you neglect yourself.
When you flop, he never splits with you— except what he has.
When you achieve success— all he wants of it, is to know it.
He is the best press agent because he doesn't have to be paid to boost you.
He works his fingers to the bone to give you a hand.
His friendship is the kind you can't lose— even when you deserve to.
He stands behind you when you're taking bows—
and beside you when you're taking boos.
Glenn Morr

GETTING The Best OUT OF OTHERS

One of the biggest problems managers encounter is not the lack of opportunities for the really motivated, but the lack of motivated people who are prepared to take advantage of those opportunities.

In reading an article the other day by Buck Rodgers and Irv Levey, they adequately describe that the most common problem facing managers is finding motivated people ready to take advantage of opportunity.

But in analyzing the situation, there really is no shortage of people who have intelligence and ability for success - even spectacular success - The problem lies in that too few of them perform at that superior level they are capable of.

Some of it is understandable. There's been too little healthy pressure put on most people to get them to stretch their potential. There's been pressure all right, but the wrong kind of pressure. It comes from frightened supervisors, who worry more about protecting their turf and their position than about getting the best out of their people or themselves.

Therefore, how do you avoid mediocrity? The first step along the way is to raise the level of your own performance and encourage those you care about or work with to do the same. If you feel good about yourself, chances are the effects will rub off onto others.

It has been said that disrespect for the individual may be the costliest long term error a company can make! Respect, on the other hand, is one of the greatest motivators for a superior performance.

Getting the best out of others begins with getting the best out of yourself.

What is Class?

*C*lass never runs scared. It is sure-footed and confident in the knowledge that you can meet life head on and handle whatever comes along.

Class never makes excuses. It takes its lumps and learns from past mistakes.

Class is considerate of others. It knows that good manners is nothing more than it series of petty sacrifices.

Class is doing your best against the very best, under the worst possible conditions.

Class bespeaks an aristocracy that has nothing to do with ancestors or money. The most affluent blue-blood can be totally without class while the descendant of a Welsh miner may ooze class from every pore.

Class never tries to build itself up by tearing others down. Class is already up and need not strive to look better by making others look worse.

Class can "walk with kings and keep its virtue, and talk with crowds and keep the common touch." Everyone is comfortable with the person who has class—because he is comfortable with himself.

Relaxing Your Body

Your body and the way it feels has such an important role in your ability to reach your fullest potential. Almost always, the better you feel the better you work; the more creative you are, the more determined you become.

It is really amazing, but relaxing your body is actually relaxing your mind. It is just another bit of evidence of the role that the mind plays in all phases of our lives.

Here are seven suggestions for relaxing your body and as you will see, they all start with the mind:

1. Think Kind Thoughts— Including about people you may not like or a job or duty that you have to perform but don't necessarily enjoy.

2. Clear Your Mind of all Negative Thinking— rid it of thoughts of worry, annoyance, resentment, guilt, and prejudices. Pretend you have a vacuum cleaner sweeping them out.

3. Think Only About Right Now— don't worry about the future or let something from the past bother or upset you. When you are relaxing, you don't need to worry about decision making.

4. Put Your Mind into a Tranquil Mood— think of being in a quiet place where it is peaceful and your mind and body can relax.

5. At Bedtime, Do Not Plan Tomorrow in Detail— if necessary, outline your day for tomorrow with some notes, but then return to happy thoughts and reaching your sleep potential.

6. If You Have Trouble Sleeping, Discontinue Your Thoughts of Problems and Concerns— you may consider watching a pleasant TV show, have light conversation or reflect with some spiritual thinking or reading.

7. Think Positively— Think about having a relaxing dinner or lunch or good night's sleep.

Relaxing the mind is the first and most important step in relaxing your body.

WATCH WHAT YOU SAY!

In the course of your conversation each and every day,
Think twice, try to be careful of what you have to say;
Your remarks may be picked up by someone's listening ear,
You may be surprised at what some people think they hear.

Things that you innocently say, or try to portray,
Can be changed, and greatly exaggerated along the way;
Many stories change for the worse as they are retold,
So try to keep any questionable remarks "on hold,"

May I give all of you some very sound advice?
When you speak to others. say something nice;
Try to say good things, regardless of who is around,
If you have nothing good to say, don't utter a sound.

You may find thai an innocent remark, in the end,
May lose you a close and valued friend.

Henry Lesser

ACTING TOGETHER

"People acting together as a group can accomplish things which no individual acting alone could ever hope to bring about."
Franklin Roosevelt

An Iowa farmer was out working his fields one day while the mother sat their two-year old daughter down Just long enough to hang some clothes on the line to dry. No sooner did she get done and turn around when the young child had disappeared. She called and called, but the child did not answer.

In a panic, she found her husband and he too began yelling her name and started into the fields looking for their daughter. After a good bit of the afternoon, the family called the local police who joined the search but with no luck. Soon, by word of mouth, townspeople heard of the terror and began coming to join in with the hope of locating the lost child. As night passed into morning there was still no sign of the child. By now the news had played the story on TV and radio and people from nearby towns began arriving and scattered all through the fields looking for the young girl. Another night was closing in and fear was greatly growing in the hearts of all.

Then one of the townspeople said, "We have about a thousand people here with us now. Why don't we join hands and form a large chain and comb the field? We can't miss her that way." Then they joined hands and a few hundred yards out the, child was located; cold and hungry, but safe.

Life can be so much more profitable to us all if we will just all learn to come together and join hands.

Success is like a blackboard; when you make your mark in the world, watch out for the guys with the erasers.

Critics. I don't think it matters what profession you are in, you are going to meet and be confronted by critics.

It has always been amazing to me that critics generally have never walked a mile in the shoes of those they criticize, yet they still don't hesitate to pass harsh words of criticism.

I can't help but think back to the talented and gifted performer Nat King Cole, who, like all of the rest of us could not escape the nasty sword and pen of the critic.

Nat King Cole once said. "The way I figure it, there are two kinds of people in the world. About 98% are in one category. They sit along the sidelines and watch the fox hunt. They applaud whoever catches the fox and then they either boo or knock those who fail to catch the fox. Now, I'm in the 2%. I don't always catch the fox and when I don't, I hear about it. But I'd rather go to the hunt than just observe it and talk about it or write about it."

The critics are out there. You have to know that whenever you hit the streets of life. Don't let them hold you back or even slow you down. Who made them experts anyway? Use the harsh words of critics as gasoline to fuel goals.

Don't let the people over on the sidelines spoil your fun as you hunt for the fox.

DALE BROWN

EXCELLENCE

Preparing more than others care to or expect,
practicing more often than the average person believes is necessary,
believing in the quality of every moment, every day and every guest
—this is what excellence is all about.

And it comes from striving, maintaining the highest standards, the highest beliefs,
looking after the smallest detail and using the basics, and going the extra mile.
Excellence means caring—caring enough about making a difference—
It means making a special effort to do more than is asked
and to expect more of oneself.

O f t e n
our fear of failure is
the cause for the lack of success.

Our society almost dictates that we become obsessed with success and victory. But have you ever asked yourself what exactly is success? Is it wealth, power, prestige, and fame? For some yes– temporarily - but in the end they find no happiness or fulfillment in this application.

We as humans don't understand or handle failure very well, but it is an inevitable part of the human condition. Therefore, we must learn to harness our fear of failure and learn from our mistakes.

Face it, we are so busy trying to achieve our fleeting moment of success that we often forget the lasting lessons of failure. We often view our failures as an end to all means. Instead, we should use our failures as to master the task the next time, remembering that a failure in one direction is the only road to mastery in others. Few people ever learn from success.

Success is having the courage to believe in yourself and not to let fear control your life. But, rather looking for ways to overcome those very fears.

Therefore, the first step in conquering our fear of failure is to first determine what our definition of success is.

Real success is the old cliche of knowing that you have done your best. A successful person is one who is productive to the peak of his or her capacity and who is comfortable with his or herself.

This sounds simplistic, but is not easily accepted. You see, in the end it is the person with self respect that is at peace with himself. All the money, fame, or glory in the world won't bring these gifts. Winning or losing is not the goal to the person with self respect. It is the journey itself.

"Remember it's not your IQ that counts,
it's your FQ– your failure quotient."
Bob Richards

TEN COMMANDMENTS OF HUMAN RELATIONS

Many times our lack of understanding is caused by our lack of communication.

1. **SPEAK TO PEOPLE.** There is nothing so nice as a cheerful word of greeting.

2. **SMILE AT PEOPLE.** It takes 72 muscles to frown, only 14 to smile.

3. **CALL PEOPLE BY NAME.** The sweetest music to anyone's ears is the sound of their own name.

4. **BE FRIENDLY AND HELPFUL.** If you would have friends, be a friend

5. **BE CORDIAL.** Speak and act if everything you do is genuine pleasure.

6. **BE GENUINELY INTERESTED IN PEOPLE.** You can like almost everybody if you try.

7. **BE GENEROUS** with praise- cautious with criticism.

8. **BE CONSIDERATE** with feelings of others. There are usually three sides to a controversy: Your side, the other fellow's side and the right side.

9. **BE ALERT** to give service. What counts most in life is what we do for others.

10. **ADD TO ALL OF THIS** a good sense of humor, a big dose of patience and a dash of humility, and you will be rewarded many-fold.

Manager Magazine

THE STRENGTH OF TOGETHERNESS

Coming together is a beginning; keeping together is progress: working together is success.

Henry Ford

One day a father called his seven sons together so that he could teach them a valuable lesson that would help them throughout life. He wanted to demonstrate what the strength of togetherness meant.

He had already gathered a bundle of seven sticks which he had carefully tied together with a string. One by one, he asked each of his seven sons to take the bundle and to try and break it. And one by one, each of the sons took their very best shot at breaking the bundle, but all failed.

At this point, the father took out a knife and cut the string and then distributed a single stick to each of the seven sons. He then repeated his request to his sons that they break the single stick in their hand, and this time each son broke the stick in their possession with great ease.

Once all the sticks had been broken, the father looked at his seven sons and said, "When you boys work together in a spirit of harmony, you resemble the bundle of sticks, and no one can defeat you; but when you quarrel among yourselves, anyone can defeat you one at a time."

DALE BROWN

Goal setting is a very important characteristic in all successful people. But, there is more to goal setting than just sitting down and saying, "Hey, I want to do this." You must have a plan of action and a burning desire that will spark a total commitment.

At the very young age of 15, John Goddard sat down and made a list of all of the things he wanted to do during his lifetime. That list totaled 127 goals. He wanted to write a book, run a five-minute mile, dive in a submarine, sail around the world, climb Mount Everest and take a boat up the Nile.

At the age of 26, Goddard was found at the beginning of the Nile River. The local government had warned him that his goal of making the 4,000 mile journey was an impossible one. During the trip, Goddard and his party was met with a number of obstacles including hippo attacks, bouts with malaria, blinding sand storms, miles of dangerous rapids, and a chase by rifle-shooting river bandits. But, in the end it was because of his determination and grit that he finally sailed into the Mediterranean Sea.

Goddard has now met 105 of the 127 goals at the age of 60, and who's to say he won't meet his 105th goal—visiting the moon!

John Goddard has proven that obstacles are only those frightful things you see when you take your eyes off the goal.

Anything is possible with goal setting and the burning desire of determination.

OVERCOMING PROBLEMS

Before you begin anything worthwhile, obstacles will swarm to confront you. If you start counting the obstacles, you'll never stop counting them. Once you start, however, you won't stop to count"

Earl Nightingale

It doesn't matter who you are or where you're from or what occupation you hold, you are going to run into obstacles. No matter how hard you try to avoid them they will always pop up on the road to success. Henry Ford, once said, "Most people spend more time and energy going around problems than in trying to solve them". Oh how true are these words. If we could focus those energies on solving instead of running away from our problems, they really wouldn't seem to be so final after all.

So how do you begin the process? Well, first look at your problems as not obstacles but hurdles you must jump over. Think of the hurdles as a challenge or an opportunity to win the race.

That's what a women named Mary Gord-Lewis did.

Mary was diagnosed with dyslexia, which is an impairment of the ability to read, often as the result of genetic defect or brain injury. Coming from a tough environment. Mary was also a street fighter, which also led her to a period in her life where she got caught up in petty theft, alcohol and even drugs. At age 16, Mary still could not read. She gave birth and raised two children out of wedlock on her own. After the second childbirth, she suffered with high blood pressure, five cardiac arrests and even a stroke. That stroke was so severe that she had to learn to talk and read all over again. But as Oliver Wendell Holmes once said, "What lies behind us, what lies ahead of us, is of very little importance when it's compared to what lies within us." Proof is in that when speaking to Mary today, her full name will read, Mary Gord-Lewis, MD.

Use your stumbling blocks as stepping stones to something better.

THE ROLE MODEL

Children learn what they live.

In his memoirs, General Robert E. Lee thought back to a moment when he realized that he was a role model for his very own son.

Lee decided to take his son on a winter walk through the countryside that was covered with new fallen snow. Hand in hand, the two took off on their journey. Soon, however, the boy dropped back and when his father looked over his shoulder he saw his son placing his little feet in the footprints already made by his father's boots.

Upon seeing this. Lee wrote, "It behooves me to walk very straight, when the Little fellow is already following in my tracks.

THINK LIKE A WINNER

"The most important discovery of my century is that you can change a man's life if you change his mental attitude".

William James

A winner is always ready to tackle something new
...a loser is prone to believe it can't be done.

A winner isn't afraid of competition
...a loser excuses himself with the idea that the competition beat him out.

A winner knows he's sometimes wrong and is willing to admit his mistakes
...a loser can usually find someone to blame.

A winner is challenged by a new problem
...a loser doesn't want to face it.

A winner is decisive
...a loser frustrates himself with indecision.

A winner realizes there is no time like the present to get a job done
...a loser is prone to procrastinate with the hope that things will be better tomorrow.

A winner thinks positively, acts positively, and lives positively
...a loser usually has a negative attitude and a negative approach to everything.

*If you want to be a winner—
think like a winner,
act like a winner
and sooner than you think
you will be a winner*

DALE BROWN

BIG ME
LITTLE ME

Failure will never overtake you if your determination to succeed is strong enough.

You know, as I look at successful people and study them through my readings, one of the most common characteristics that keeps resurfacing time and time again is persistence.

Almost every success story begins with hard work followed by a strong determination to overcome the failures and obstacles along the way. That determination is simply called persistence.

To quote Calvin Coolidge;
"Nothing in the world can take the place of persistence. Talent will not do it. nothing is more common than unsuccessful men with talent. Genius will not; unrewarded genius is almost a proverb. Education will not; the world is full of educated derelicts. Persistence and determination alone are omnipotent. The slogan 'press on' has solved and will always solve the problems of the human race."

But there is also more than just having the will or determination to succeed. Along the way you will be tempted by your human weakness and desires. You see, in everyone there is a higher and lower self and it is the drive of your persistence that will determine which self will prevail.

For example, the great Italian tenor, Enrico Caruso, believed that inside him were two personalities that he named "Big Me" and "Little Me." Caruso felt that these two personalities were always doing battle within him. Big Me was the one that rose to the occasion to meet all challenges, hurdle all obstacles and felt destined for greatness. Little Me was the pouter, the negative thinker and the one that was always doubtful.

But the only thing that Caruso felt that enabled "Big Me" to defeat "Little Me" the majority of the time was simply persistence.

The difference between a successful person and others is not a lack of strength, not a lack of knowledge, but rather a lack of will and persistence.

Turn Your Greatest WEAKNESS Into Your Greatest STRENGTH

At the age of 2, in a freak accident Chad Howey spent 10 dreadful minutes under water. The doctors at his hospital used the terminology "cold water drowning" to describe his very serious condition. At two years of age all that he had known was separated from his mind, as if a cassette tape had been erased.

As he grew older, Chad's motor skill and mental capabilities began to deteriorate and it became increasingly more difficult for him to keep up with his classmates. But, what hurt him the most was the ridicule from his classmates when he read.

It was then, at 10 years of age, that Chad decided he was going to flip over his life's developments, and turn his greatest weakness into his greatest strength. He enrolled in a speed-reading course.

If you are an average reader, you probably read about 250 words per minute and comprehend around 75%. A speed-reading course can sometimes double that and even triple it, and there have been some people that could take in 1,000 words per minute.

Well, Chad Howey took it to the limit. At age 10, with all of his determination, Chad could read 9,000 to 10,000 words per minute and do it with a 90% comprehension rate! Proof that Chad didn't give up on his goal because he never gave up on himself.

The true story of Chad Howey should remind you to act to overcome your weakness and your weakness will become your strength.

THE POWER OF CHOICE

The greatest power that a person possesses is the power to choose.

Within each of us there lies a power. A power that can determine our happiness and success. A power that can help us realize our dreams. That power is the power to choose.

Basically, we have a choice every day on how we will react to life. And, it's up to us if that choice will be positive or negative.

We can be anything we want to be just by making a conscious decision to choose. William James once said, "Compared with what we ought to be, we are only half awake. The human individual lives usually far within his limits; he possesses powers of various sorts which we habitually fail to use".

We have a choice everyday on how we will react to life. We decide on whether or not to pursue an issue or ignore it; to persevere in times of trouble, or to buckle under. We have the power to choose to go for a life-long goal or be content to stay on the same level forever. We must decide whether we'll give it our 100% best or merely half try. It is our decision to be honest and good, rather than crooked and mean; to be eager and hardworking; instead of dull and lazy. In the face of the test, it is what we do with our power to choose that determines the potential quality of our lives.

Take charge of your life. You have the power to choose– It's up to **YOU**!

Sometime ago Norman Vincent Peale wrote a book entitled, **"Enthusiasm Makes The Difference."** In it, he detailed a formula that may help you put everyday in a positive, uplifting perspective.

"Think a Good Day" If you have a positive image of the day before it unfolds, it will help get you going in the right direction.

"Thank a Good Day." Give thanks for a good day in advance and that positive imagery helps make it so.

"Plan a Good Day." Put some positive things into your day to help get it on the right track and keep it there.

"Put Good into the Day." Put good thoughts, good attitudes and good actions into a day and they will make the day good.

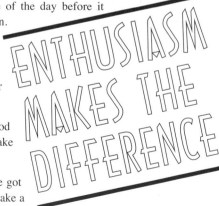

Fill the day with enthusiasm. Give the day all you've got and it will give it right back to you. Enthusiasm can make a difference in a day, a job and in your life. Think a good day and you will have one.

Our days are few, so make the best of them. *"Enthusiasm makes the difference"*.

The Importance Of <u>Good</u> Health

There are many mental factors that are involved in being successful and happy.

Positive attitudes, being persistent, determination and the importance of goal setting are a few. However, there is a physical element that is also involved in being successful and happy, and that is your health. The great thing about your health is that you have a great deal of control as to how healthy you are by the habits you keep, and the key word here is habits.

We are the ones in charge of whether we exercise or not, whether we eat properly or not, or whether we poison our bodies. Here is an example of what I am talking about and the effects involved.

In a survey of approximately 7,000 people in Alameda County California. The research doctors found that the healthiest people seemed to have developed seven basic habits:

The amazing thing, and this is important to remember and somewhat the moral of the story, the people with those seven habits had a life expectancy of 11 years longer than others.

A healthy body does lead to a healthier mind.

1 They never smoke cigarettes

2 They have regular physical activity

3 They use alcohol moderately or never

4 They get 7 to 8 hours of sleep each night

5 They maintain their proper weight

6 They eat breakfast, and

7 They avoid eating between meals

Attitude Counts

It's not your aptitude that counts in life, it's your attitude.

As Charles Swindoll once said, "Our attitudes control our lives. They are a secret power working 24 hours a day, for good or bad. It is of paramount importance that we know how to harness and control this great force."

"The longer you live, the more you realize the importance of attitude on life. Attitude is more important than facts, more important than the past, than education, than money, than circumstances, than failures, than successes, than what other people think or say or do. It Is more important than appearance or skill. It will make or break a team, a company, a home.The remarkable thing is we have a choice every day regarding the attitude we embrace for that day. We cannot change our past ... we cannot change the inevitable. The only thing we can do is play on the one string we have, and that is our attitude. Life is 10 percent what happens to us and 90 percent how we react to it. We are in charge of our attitudes and we are the ones who have the choice.

We have a choice every morning when we wake up, if it will be a good day or a bad day, if we'll work hard or be lazy, or if we'll be kind or selfish. It is our choice.

Sure sometimes there are circumstances beyond our control, but we do have a choice in how we'll react to it. The same is true when searching for success. If you think a task can't be done chances are it won't get done. But if you think positive, chances are your results will be positive. Think about it - "All that man achieves and all that he fails to achieve is a direct result of his own thoughts".

Your attitude does control your life, the choice is up to you!

HARD WORK & PERSEVERANCE

"Nobody's more apt to set the world on fire than the fellow who bums the midnight oil".

Basically, there are three types of people in the hunt for success. There are those who just want to roll out of the bed and be successful. Then, there are those who are so busy learning the tricks of the trade they never really learn the trade. And finally, there are those who are willing to pay the price for success. That price is hard work and perseverance. And, I can't think of two characteristics that are so closely related to excellence.

But, work ethic and drive are not traits that come easy. You must feel compelled from within to experience their value.

You see the main reason why most people don't recognize the opportunity for success is because it usually comes disguised as hard work. These people are not willing to sacrifice and risk failure for the very thing they want the most. But without hard work, sacrifice and perseverance, their dreams will remain just that– a dream. You have to want it!

A parable that exemplifies this drive is the story of the young man who was impatient for knowledge and success. So, he decided to seek the counsel of Socrates, the famous Greek philosopher. Boldly the student asked, "Socrates, how can I obtain knowledge and success?".

Socrates then proceeded to lead the student to water and suddenly grabbed him by the throat and pulled him under the water. The young man struggled and fought with all he had before finally pushing his way out of the water. Stunned and amazed he said, "What's the matter with you? I asked you how to acquire wisdom and success and you tried to kill me!"

Socrates calmly replied, "When you want wisdom and success as much as you wanted air, you will acquire it."

The man who wakes up and finds himself successful hasn't been asleep.

YOU CAN'T AFFORD
THE LUXURY OF A
NEGATIVE THOUGHT

Do you have a terrible addiction– the addiction of the negative thought?

Negative thinking is very much a disease of the mind that can effect your entire life in every phase. It is very much a habit just like those we more commonly think of such as drugs, alcohol and overeating.

Negative thinking can be just as life threatening because it can affect your body, your mind and your soul. It was once said that all man achieves and all that he fails to achieve is the direct result of his own thoughts.

To cure the negative thinking habit, take these three steps.

First, stop thinking negative thoughts. This sounds somewhat strange, but if you are thinking about something and it is negative, you need to alter the way that you think about it or stop thinking about it altogether.

Secondly, start thinking about positive aspects of your life. We all have them, some of us just don't seem to grasp onto them as well. Have a list of things that are positive written down and when you start thinking negatively, pull out that list.

Thirdly, and this is very important, associate with positive thinkers. Association plays a big part in our lives. If you want to be positive, don't hang out with negative thinkers.

Positive thoughts will produce positive results.

CHILDREN LEARN
WHAT THEY LIVE

I'd rather see a lesson than hear one any day.
I'd rather you walk with me than merely show me the way.

The eyes are a better teacher, and more willing, than the ear.
Your counsel is confusing, but examples are always clear.

I soon can learn to do it if you let me see it done.
I can see your hand in action but your tongue too fast may run.

The counsel you are giving may be very fine and true.
But I'd rather get my lesson by observing what you do.

DEDICATE YOURSELF TO A GOAL

*Approximately 95% of the world's discoveries
were made in times of deep trouble and failure.*

*I*f you are among the ninety percent of Americans who are looking for an opportunity to fail, you can become one of the ten percent who are looking for an opportunity to succeed when you first begin to set goals for your life.

*I*n setting goals, you will be able to see opportunities that you were blind to before. You will begin to recognize chances to do things that will help you to make your mark in life.

*H*istory book's reveal that an ancient block of marble was once discarded because local artisans thought it useless. One artist did not. And when Michelangelo took that slab of marble and created something beautiful, everyone stood in awe. In their amazement they asked Michelangelo how he could have created his magnificent sculpture of David out of a crude block of stone. It's simple, he replied. I just looked inside and saw the angel David screaming to get out.

*M*ichelangelo saw an opportunity where others did not.

*S*etting goals and then achieving them, one-by-one, enables a person to recognize opportunity even in the face of adversity– the same opportunity that most other people don't see. A goal is that surge inside that lifts you, pushes you, pulls you, and forces you to become the best that you can be.

*T*urn your obstacles into possibilities by dedicating yourself to a goal.

Creativity

"A man's life is dyed the color of his imagination"

Marcus Aurelius

There cannot be anything more powerful than a person's imagination. With an imagination, a person can dream without limitations. Creativity has little do with just how much you know. Creativity is a matter of looking at things differently and from a viewpoint all your own.

Philip Goldberg, a tremendous speaker on creativity, once listed a wonderful set of suggestions in order to be more creative:

1.

Look at the problem from as many different angles as possible. The problem should be defined in such a way to be manageable, neither too narrow nor too broad to work with.

2.

Write down all your thoughts and feelings about the situation. The more you can immerse yourself in the problem, the more material you will have to work with.

3.

Take in different types of information, even though some of it may seem irrelevant at the time. Apart from relevant information, you may walk through a new part of town, watch a TV show you've never watched before, browse in a section of the library where you usually don't go or start up a conversation with a stranger. As Jonathan Swift said, "Vision is the art of seeing things invisible".

4.

Practice brainstorming. To brainstorm, write down any and all possible solutions to your problem. The real trick to brainstorming is that you write down whatever comes to mind regardless of how silly, useless or meaningless it may seem. Remember, ideas are funny little things. They won't work unless you do.

YOU ARE AS BIG AS YOU THINK

You are as big as you think, and if you don't believe that statement then listen to this story about John and Greg Rice.

These two twins were born as dwarfs. Shortly after birth, they were abandoned by their parents because the young couple wouldn't accept the responsibility of raising a pair of clubfoot dwarfs.

Nine months later they were taken in by a couple. But while in grade school, within two years, both of those adults died. Still, the twins maintained unbelievable positive attitudes and set a goal in high school that by their 10-year class reunion they would be millionaires.

They started out as door-to-door salesmen and soon ended up owning a successful company and becoming the millionaires that they dreamed of as youngsters. They now spend most of their time lecturing around the country on the topic of, you guessed it - **Thinking Big.**

In their spare time they can be found sailing their own boat, playing tennis on a regulation size court where they can barely see over the net, or swimming, which is something that experts said dwarfs were physically unable to do.

Thank goodness that John and Greg Rice didn't listen to the experts outline their limitations. They realized that the difference between a successful person and others, is not a lack of height, but rather a lack of will.

They didn't let the obstacle of their physical abilities interfere with their will and drive to succeed.

You are as big as you think you are.

HOW TO TELL A
WINNER

How do you tell a winner from a loser?

▲ A Winner says, *"Let's find out"*, a loser says. *"Nobody knows"*

▲ When a Winner makes a mistake he says, "*I was wrong*"; when a loser makes a mistake, he says *"It wasn't my fault"*.

▲ A Winner credits his "*good luck*" for winning - even though it isn't good luck; a loser blames his *"bad luck"* for losing - even though it isn't bad luck.

▲ A Winner is nearly as afraid of losing as a loser is secretly afraid of winning.

▲ A Winner works harder than a loser, and has more time; a loser is always too busy to do what is necessary.

▲ A Winner goes through a problem; a loser goes around it, and never gets past it.

▲ A Winner makes commitments; a loser makes promises.

▲ A Winner listens; a loser just waits until it's his turn to talk.

▲ A Winner says, *"I'm good but not a good as I ought to be"*; a loser says, *"I'm not as bad as a lot of other people"*.

▲ A Winner respects those who are superior to him, and tries to learn something from them; a loser resents those who are superior to him, and tries to find chinks in their armor.

▲ A Winner feels responsible for more than his job, a loser says, *"I only work here"*

▲ A Winner doesn't care who gets the credit and will take the blame, a loser takes all the credit but passes the blame.

▲ So, if you want to be a winner, think like a winner, act like a winner... and sooner than you think, you will be a winner.

THE BUILDER

There can be not progress, nor achievement, without sacrifice.

In constructing the building of life, there are 3 basic types of jobs involved in the construction. In observing a group of men tearing a building down, I began to realize that what would only lake a few days to destroy, took a builder many years to plan and construct. And I thought to myself as I began to walk away, that the building and tearing down of this once great monument was similar to what we experience in life.

You see, in constructing the building of life, there are three jobs or three types of people involved in the process. The first type builds and plans the blocks of life, the second observes the construction of it, and the third tears down the builder's dream.

Ask yourself which job you would choose. Obviously, tearing down or observing is much easier; that's why so many people are eager and willing to take the job. The pay is not as good as the builder's, but, hey, you don't have to work as hard. And there is nothing to risk.

Whereas the builder's job may pay more, few people are willing to sacrifice for the job. The main reason is that a builder's job is much more difficult to master and therefore, requires much more work, sacrifice and persistence. What people don't know is that, in the end, a builder's reward is the realization of the dream. Few people are willing to sacrifice in order to achieve excellence.

Which job would you choose?

"If we were really aware of our own powers, we would live in a continuous state of awe".

Earl Nightingale

One day while passing a wealthy merchant's home, an old stone cutter imagined how great it would be to become the merchant and possess his wealth. Then, magically, he was transformed into that merchant. Shortly afterwards, he saw some merchants bow down a king. He than dreamed of being the king; again, he was transformed. Soon following, he had trouble seeing due to the strength of the rays of the mighty sun. He thought how powerful he would be if he was the sun overlooking all and spreading heat and sunshine. He then became the sun.

THE STONE CUTTER

From his spot high in the sky, he radiated sunshine for all until clouds passed under him and blocked his rays. Realizing this power in the clouds he wished he were one, and then he became one. Now he felt himself moving through the power of the wind and thus he began to blow. And blow he did, tearing down houses and buildings and pulling trees up from the ground. Then he came upon a large immovable boulder and no matter how hard he blew, he just couldn't budge it. It was now that he realized that this great rock was the strongest most powerful force in the world and he wished to become one; and so he became this great rock.

At about this time, he felt a strong hammering, pounding force hitting him and he found himself breaking up. It was at this time that he looked and saw another stone cutter.

"There is always hope for tomorrow if you believe in yourself today"

THE COMEBACK
of
TOMMY JOHN

Tommy John was consistently one of the top pitchers year-in and year-out in major league baseball. During his career he pitched for Tommy Lasorda with the LA Dodgers, as well as pitching for the New York Yankees.

One night while pitching for the Dodgers in Montreal. John felt a sharp pain in his elbow that was so severe that he could not even toss a ball, let alone pitch. What the team doctors discovered was a torn ligament in his arm that had also separated from his muscles.

His hand was actually drawing up because the nerves leading to the hand were dead.

The next couple of years found the hand getting worse to the point where it was nearly totally paralyzed. It was written that his great officer was over. Then John accidently heard a speaker talk of the power of self-belief. It greatly inspired him and he began to work daily with his sights set on pitching again. The training was torture but, his goal bad been burned in his soul and he would let nothing stop him. Following a year of rehab and tremendous work, not to mention excruciating pain, John came back and pitched for Lasorda's Dodgers and won 20 games leading the team in victories.

MENTAL TOUGHNESS
and the
GOLD MEDAL

*Life's battles don't always go to the
swiftest and strongest man;
But sooner or later the one who wins,
is the man who thinks he can.*

Nothing could be closer to the truth. You have to believe in your abilities and be persistent.

A great example is Bruce Jenner. the Decathlon Gold Medal winner of the 1976 Olympics. Jenner has said repeatedly that, while he was active in sports in high school, he never really excelled in one particular area. Even in Olympic competition, Jenner was smart enough to know his weaknesses, saying that his greatest asset was not his physical ability. However, he recognized the importance of his mental capabilities saying that he "honestly felt he was mentally tougher than the guys he competed against in the Olympics." He felt it was the critical element that helped him perform so well in pressure situations.

Most sports psychologists will agree that there is a certain intangible that lifts some athletes to higher levels than others, and that special something is more mental than physical. Bruce Jenner was not necessarily the swiftest or strongest man; he won because he thought he could.

You don't have to be a competitor for the decathlon Gold Medal to get this formula to work for you.

One person with a belief is equal to a force of 99 who only have interests.

A SHORT COURSE IN
HUMAN RELATIONS

Our ability to communicate with each other is such a vital measure for success in anything we do whether we are at the work place, at home with the family or at church.

Too many times in our efforts to communicate with each other, we think only of ourselves, we look to gain a pat on the back or we tend to downgrade others in hopes of uplifting ourselves. We should look to build and to bond when we speak, and in doing that - a short course in human relations.

The 6 most important words in the English language:

"I ADMIT I MADE A MISTAKE."

The 5 most important words:
"YOU DID A GOOD JOB."

The 4 most important words:
"WHAT IS YOUR OPINION?"

The 3 most important words:
"IF YOU PLEASE."

The one most important word:
"WE"

The least important word:
"I"

DEFEATING THE FEAR OF
FAILURE

There are so many obstacles out there that keep us from reaching our potential. But, none may be as great as the fear of failure. So many people out there don't even attempt to reach their potential because they are afraid of stumbling or getting knocked down along the way.

Take the story of Ron Guidry, also known as Louisiana Lightning because of his powerful fastball. But he was once afraid of failure and almost quit on his career before it even took off.

As had been the case in previous years, Guidry was being sent down to the minors because the administration just didn't think he had what it look to play major league baseball. Guidry, rejected, discouraged and feeling like a failure, packed his bags and headed home.

But on his drive back, something clicked.

Would he live to regret that he gave up his life long dream just because of one more set back? He had overcome failure before, so why was this latest obstacle any different? His decision was made.

And before it was over. Ron Guidry became not only the winner of the Cy Young award, as the best pitcher in the major league, but he helped the New York Yankees win the World Series.

You see, if it had not been for that long drive back home, Ron may have never lived his dream because it was only then in his darkest hour, that he reminded himself that true courage was facing failure when he was the most afraid.

Sometimes in our darkest hour our brightest moments are right around the corner, if we just have the courage to keep traveling.

THE JOURNEY

"A young man searches for happiness: In addition to searching for truth.

He tries to discover true peace.

During the early days of his youth.

He climbs the highest mountain,
He covers uncharted ground,
Expending much of his energy,
In hopes the answer will be found.

After all the stones are turned over, And the searcher has slowed stride;
The older man finally realizes,
That the answer was always inside.

As we live each day to the fullest, We must not forget to recall: "It is better to have tried and failed, Than to not have tried at all."

Now that our Journey is almost over, The answer is a revelation.
The significance is the JOURNEY, And not the destination."

Chris Neck

IT'S NOT YOUR BACK GROUND, IT'S YOUR BACKBONE

It's not your background that counts, it's your backbone.

So often, one of the most common excuses used by people falling short of their potential is that they didn't have very much starting out. Their family was poor. They didn't have a father. They didn't get a break.

It's a good thing that a young boy named Johnny didn't fall back on these excuses.

After his father died, his mother was left to support the family. She worked four different jobs by waiting tables, cleaning offices, working in a bakery, and delivering coal, but she just barely managed to make ends meet in the war-depressed years of the 40's.

John wanted to do the impossible by his family standards and go on to a major college, hopefully to play football, But no big school scholarships came his way. He was too slow and too small. After a successful career at a small college, he decided he wanted to play in the NFL, but was quickly cut by Pittsburgh.

While working in a construction company, he continued to work on his game and actually played semi-pro ball for $6.00 a game. All this time he was writing to other pro teams, until he finally received an invitation to tryout for the Baltimore Colts.

That little Johnny grew up to be John Unitas and is considered by some as the best quarterback ever and has a place in the hall-of-fame. He constantly led the league in passing and led his team to championships. All because he failed to rest on all the excuses that he had available, but didn't want to use.

After all, it's not your background that counts, but your backbone.

"They say this... they say that... it makes me wonder where I'm at!
Identify those known as They and I'll have more respect for what they say"

"In the battle of life, it is not the critic who counts; not the man who points out how the

strong man stumbled, or where the doer of the deed could have done better. The credit belongs to the man who is actually in the arena; whose face is marred by dust and sweat and blood; who strives valiantly; who errs and comes short again because there is no effort without error and shortcomings; who does actually strive to do the deeds; who knows the great enthusiasm, the great devotion, spends himself in a worthy cause; who at best knows in the end triumph of high achievement; and who at worst if he fails, at least fails while daring greatly, so that his place shall never be with those cold and timid souls who have tasted neither victory nor defeat".

Theodore Roosevelt

The Bottom Line

FACE IT...
Nobody owes you a living, What you achieve or fail to achieve in your lifetime is directly related to what you do or fail to do.
No one chooses his parents or childhood but you can choose your own direction.
Everyone has problems and obstacles to overcome but that too is relative to each individual.

NOTHING IS CARVED IN STONE...
You can change anything in your life, if you want to badly enough.

EXCUSES ARE FOR LOSERS...
Those who take responsibility for their actions are the real winners in life. Winners meet life's challenges head on, knowing there are no guarantees, and give it all they've got.
And never think it's too late or too early to begin,
Time plays no favorites and will pass whether you act or not.

TAKE CONTROL OF YOUR LIFE...
Dare to dream and take risks... Compete.
If you aren't willing to work for your goals don't expect others to.

BELIEVE IN YOURSELF!

LIFE'S BANK ACCOUNT

Most everyone has a banking and or savings account at a local financial institution. What you don't know is that you also have a savings account in your soul. That's right— your life is somewhat like a bank.

We all know how a checking account operates. You take an amount of money, deposit it into the bank and it stores there until you are ready to withdraw it. If you put $5 in the bank, then they will let you take out $5. If you put $10,000 in the bank then they will let you take out $10,000. You get out of the bank what you put into it and the same is true of life.

Just as a bank needs a committed depositor base to be successful, so does the bank of life. Are you committed to depositing the investments of hard work & sacrifice necessary to realize the dividends of success?

Oh, I'm not talking about material success. I'm referring to the rewards of doing a job well, helping a friend in need, providing a home of love to your family. These things are what true success is about.

Albert Einstein once said, *"Try not to become a man of success, but rather try to become a man of value"*.

Isn't that how we should look at our bank of life. If we put in love, sacrifice, and charity... in return, we'll receive dividends ten fold. Because if you give, so shall you receive. Life really is what you put into it.

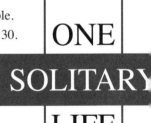

ONE

SOLITARY

LIFE

☩ He was born in an obscure village, the child of ordinary people.

☩ He grew up in a small town in a carpenter shop until He was 30.

☩ Then for three years He was an itinerant preacher.

☩ He never wrote a book.

☩ He never held an office.

☩ He never had a wife or owned a house.

☩ He didn't go to college.

☩ He did none of the things one usually associates with greatness.

☩ He had no credentials but Himself.

☩ He was only thirty-three when the tide of public opinion turned against Him.

☩ His friends ran away.

☩ He was turned over to His enemies and went through the mockery of a trial.

☩ He was nailed to a cross between two thieves.

☩ While He was dying, His executioners gambled for His clothing, the only property He had on earth.

☩ When He was dead, He was laid in a borrowed grave through the pity of a friend.

☩ Nineteen centuries have come and gone, and today He is the central figure of the human race and the leader of mankind's progress.

☩ All the armies that ever marched, all the navies that ever sailed, all the parliaments that have ever sat, all the kings that ever reigned put together, have not affected the life of man on the earth as much as the One Solitary Life.

DALE BROWN

TOGETHERNESS AND TEAMWORK CAN CONQUER ALL

Nineteen of the twenty-one most notable civilizations in the history of the world have crumbled or died from within.

How often do teams, organizations, and even families fail to meet their potential or never find true happiness and success because they let petty jealousies and minor differences interfere with their common goal?

Take history for example. One of the greatest dynasties the world has ever known was the Roman Empire. Their untouchable empire spanned centuries. It seemed that nothing could ever destroy it. But, eventually the Roman Empire did fall. But it was not because of outside factors. The empire fell from within its own ranks.

Even today we continue this legacy in our own lives. And when a team or company is successful, we wonder how they do it. Bill Russell of the Boston Celtics, who won 11 NBA titles as a player and two as coach, has been asked that same question of his teams and his response went something like this:

"There were Jews, Catholics, Protestants on our team. White men and black men on our team. The one thing we shared in common was an Irish name.

One of our secrets was that we never had any cliques. You might see me, the rebel, out one night with whites, another night with blacks, and a third night with whites and blacks. We simply considered ourselves a proud group of men who bore the distinction of being something no one else could be in our sport— the champions of the world."

You see, what drove them to excellence wasn't the color of their skin, or the selfishness of their egos. In fact they had nothing in common at all but the cause of the team. They simply looked at all of their differences and blended them into their greatest strength.

Togetherness and teamwork can conquer all adversity. But, dissension from within can crumble even the greatest of empires.

General George S. Patton in his war memoirs recounted the individual courage and sacrifice of a common soldier.

"I decorated Private Harold A. Garman, of the 5th Infantry Division, with the Medal of Honor. Garman was attached to a medical unit in one of the battalions that was forced to cross the Sauer River in heavy combat. During the action, a boat with three walking wounded, paddled by two engineers, started back and was caught by German machine-gun fire in the middle of the river. The engineers and one of the walking wounded jumped overboard and swam for shore. The other two wounded jumped overboard, but were too weak to swim and clung to the boat. The boat, still under a hail of bullets drifted toward the German shore. But, with little regard for his own safety, Private Garman swam out and pushed the boat to our side. I asked him why he did it, and he looked surprised and said, "Well, someone had to.""

HIGH ACHIEVEMENT FACTORS

*"All that we are is the result of what we have thought;
it is founded on our thoughts, it is made up of our thoughts"*

Buddha

Dr. Eugene Griessman wrote a book entitled "The Achievement Factors". He details that many of the worlds high achievers have not had extraordinary talent, but they all possessed similar characteristics. Some of those are as follows:

1. High achievers discover their vocations and their specialties. That means they find something they love doing. Have you ever noticed that people who derive so much satisfaction from their work do it well?

2. High Achievers develop competency. Doing something well is the very foundation upon which all high achievement is built. If you like your job then the nitty gritty tasks won't seem so nitty gritty after all.

3. High Achievers value and manage time well. High achievers devise little strategies to conserve time, like taking along a magazine or book to read on the plane or at the doctor's office.

4. High Achievers are persistent. They are not easily stopped if they feel they are on the right track.

5. High Achievers develop the Ability to Focus. They possess the ability to tune out static and distractions and give absolute attention to the task at hand.

6. High Achievers perceive opportunities. They are open to what is happening around them. They are always learning because they are inquisitive, questioning individuals.

7. High Achievers seize opportunities because they are willing to take risks. They never make excuses and often turn their obstacles into opportunities in which to build success.

Words to Live By...

Learn to forgive
if you are to be forgiven.

Talk bad about others
and others will think bad about you.

Try to to control the uncontrollable
and it will control you.

Think only of yourself,
and you will end up alone.

If you only see the hurdles
you'll never win the race.

Yesterday's guilt
will only turn into Tomorrow's worry.

Negative thoughts
will produce negative results.

A person with little faith
will have little hope.

Dale Brown

THE ANSWER
IN
THE PROBLEM

Every problem contains within itself the seeds of its own solutions.

So many times in life we are faced with tough times and adversity but it is the way we face up to such difficult periods that can actually make the difference in success and failure.

Whenever I think of making the most of a difficult situation, I think back to the parable of the two frogs that just happened to fall into a deep jar filled with a little cream. The top of the cream was far from the jar's top, and though the frogs gave it everything they had for an extended period of time, they could not leap out.

In despair, one frog could not help but be a negative thinker and could vision nothing but thoughts of defeat.

"I know I can't get out. I know I have to die, so why not get it over with." In resignation, he sank and died.

"Sure, I may die," said the second frog. "But if I do, I'll go down kicking." And with great vigor he began to swim, thrashing about and kicking. His continued activity churned the cream into butter and, feeling solid footing, he leaped out of the jar to safety.

Often the answer is in the problem itself, so just keep kicking.

Integrity
&
President Lincoln

Integrity without knowledge is weak and useless, and knowledge without integrity is dangerous and dreadful

At the very young age of 24, Abraham Lincoln took a job working as the postmaster in a very small and quaint town in Illinois named New Salem. For all of his labor, the young Lincoln received a yearly salary of a paltry $55.70.

Remember that even though he was just 24 years of age, as well as 24 years away from entering the White House as this nation's 16th President, that the rail splitter was showing the kind of character that earned him the title of "Honest Abe."

In the year of 1836, due to a lack of business, the post office located in New Salem, Illinois was closed by the government. Several years later a government agent arrived in Washington, D.C. to settle accounts with the ex-postmaster, Abraham Lincoln. Mr. Lincoln at this time, was a struggling lawyer who was down on his luck and not doing very well.

The agent informed him that records had showed that $17 was due to the government left over from the closing of the post office. Lincoln crossed his room in his run-down office, opened an old trunk and took out a yellowed cotton rag, bound with a string. Untying it, he spread out the cloth and there was exactly $17. He had been holding it untouched for all those years, searching for the proper place to return it. "I never use any man's money but my own," he said.

Think how much greater this world would be if we all shared the same integrity as "Honest Abe."

IT'S ALL IN OUR PERCEPTION

"Minds are like parachutes; they only function when they are open"

Sir James Dewar

So much of everything that we do in life is shaped by our power of perception. Our ability to imagine events or goals in our minds before they even occur can be a powerful tool in shaping our future. However, it is also important that the perception of a goal does not interfere with the realization of that goal. In other words, sometimes our original perception can be so strong that when the end result is not exactly what we had visualized, we don't appreciate the real value of the result.

Take these examples:
On the date of October 12, 1492, a crewman aboard the Spanish sailing ship Pinta started screaming, Land! Land! Land! The captain of this great mission, Christopher Columbus, had hoped that they had found his objective, India. Unfortunately, in Columbus' perception, they had discovered two unknown continents. And, for most of his life, Columbus tried to persuade people that he had indeed discovered China.

A decade later. Amerigo Vespucci came across the same huge land mass but could only come to feel that it was nothing more than an obstacle to reaching India.

It was because of their unbending perception, that neither explorer could visualize their discoveries as positive. Columbus thought it was something it was not, and Vespucci thought it was nothing more than an obstacle. But in reality it was a land of great wealth of natural resources filled with gold and silver as well as unsettled territory with unlimited potential.

Each were so inflexible in their goals that they couldn't see past their original perceptions to understand fully just what they had done.

Perception or visualization should only be used as a guide in your quest, not an end- You must be willing to open your mind to all possibilities and be flexible enough to appreciate whatever result happens.

Forgive
─── AND ───
FORGET

"The first and worst of all frauds is to cheat yourself"
J. Baily

"Carrying a grudge is a loser's game. It is the ultimate frustration because it leaves you with more pain than you had in the first place. Recall the pain of being wronged, the hurt of being stung, cheated, demeaned. Doesn't the memory of it fuel the fire of fury again? Do you feel that hurt each time your memory lights on the people who did you wrong? Your own memory becomes a videotape within your soul that plays unending reruns of your old rendezvous with pain. Is this fair to yourself- this wretched justice of not forgiving?

The only way to heal the pain that will not heal itself is to forgive the person who hurt you. Forgiving heals your memory as you change your memory's vision. When you release the wrongdoer from the wrong, you cut a malignant tumor out of your inner life. You set a prisoner free - Yourself".

Lewis Smedes

*"An optimist is one who sees an opportunity in every difficulty-
a pessimist is one who sees a difficulty in every opportunity"*

Abraham Lincoln

"Be so strong that nothing can disturb your peace of mind. Talk health, happiness and prosperity to every person you meet. Make all your friends feel that there is something worthwhile in them. Look at the sunny side of everything and make your optimism come true. Think only of the best, work only for the best and expect only the best. Be just as enthusiastic about the success of others as you are about your own. Forget about the mistakes of the past and press on to the greater achievements of the future. Wear a cheerful countenance at all times and give every living creature you meet a smile. Give so much time to the improvement of yourself that you have no time to criticize others. Be too large for worry, too noble for anger, too strong for fear and too happy to permit the presence of trouble."

It's all in your attitude whether or not you will be an optimist or pessimist.

The Optimist Club Creed

I MAKE THE DIFFERENCE

"An individual can make a difference… a team can make a miracle"

"I make the difference. I know that what I do makes it possible for my office to run smoothly. The effort I put into my job shows up in the quality of my office's services and in my company's earnings.

I'm part of what outsiders see when they judge my organization. With every letter, every phone conversation, every personal contact, I make a statement about the caliber of service we offer. In the course of a year, I make hundreds of valuable business contacts for my company.

How I feel on a given day affects the people I work with. I help to set the tone here. I know that when I bring real enthusiasm to the job, I make a contribution few others can equal.

I also take responsibility for what bothers me—whether it's a procedure that isn't working, a practice I feel is unfair, or a person I'm having difficulty with. I do what I can to change the situation. When I can't get a situation changed, I look for ways to minimize its effect on me. Most important, I remember that I've chosen to work here, and as long as I'm here, I'll give my best.

I'm proud to be a strong, reliable member of my company's team. I know that my success, as well as the company's success, depends on it."

From the Dartnell Corporation motto

DETERMINATION

PAYS OFF IN THE LONG RUN

If you and your opponent are near equal, the deciding factor will always be determination.

There was a young man with a weak back, poor vision and one leg that was shorter than the other. Still, he had set a goal to play collegiate football and enrolled at Southern Methodist University to try to gain a spot on the roster. With a great deal of hard work combined with courage, he met his goal and played college football for the Mustangs.

After reaching one goal, he decided to set another— his second goal was to play in the National Football League. He had become a good college football player, but not an outstanding one, and was overlooked until late in the 20th round. Not many gave him a chance to make his new team, the Baltimore Colts.

But he was ever so determined. He wore a harness on his back to overcome his bad back. To overcome his short leg problem. he wore two different kinds of cleats on each foot. He was the first player in the NFL to wear contact lenses to improve his vision. Of course, his work ethic continued to excel.

By the time he had finished his career, Raymond Berry was considered one of the all-time great pass receivers in NFL history, where he also teamed with quarterback Johnny Unitas to lead the Colts to two championships. You see, Raymond Berry's story of perseverance is like that of a stone cutter hammering away at his rock perhaps 100 times without as much as a crack showing in it. Yet at the 101st blow it split in two, and he knows it wasn't the blow that did it, but all that had gone before.

"When you've exhausted all possibilities, remember this: you haven't. The solution may only be in the next blow".

THE WILL TO WIN

The will to win comes from within

There is a certain attitude related to winning that makes an individual reach their ultimate potential. That attitude is the will to win.

There are so many areas in life in which the will to win is important. When we're on the operating table, we sure want that surgeon to possess that "want-to-win" attitude. When we're in a court of law and we know we're innocent, we sure hope that lawyer wants to win. And when the fire is engulfing our home, we hope that the fire fighter has the courage to win.

How then, do you develop that will to win? First, ask yourself what are your real reasons for wanting to win? Is it for money? Is it for acknowledgement? Or is it to help others? Once you can assess the driving force of your desires, it will become easier to pursue your goal because you will have a clearer understanding.

The second factor in determining the will to win is developing a confidence to pursue it. If a person expects to win, regardless of whether they are suiting up in a basketball uniform, heading into the classroom, or stepping onto Wall Street, chances are they will win. However, be careful to know the difference between self-confidence and over confidence. The latter could be fatal.

Finally, you must be willing to work hard, make the necessary sacrifices, risk failure and make a total commitment.

It's not just one, but a combination of all of these characteristics that will create the driving force behind your will to win.

THE CIRCUS ELEPHANT

So many times we are faced with limitations that we ourselves place in front of us. Often times it comes from that thought conditioning pattern that tells us it can't be done.

A few years ago, a circus was visiting the Maravich Assembly Center and in observing the enormous elephants, I was amazed that they were tied down by a small chain and stake.

How could this be? What would cause this mammoth being of tremendous strength to be tamed so easily with so little? I asked the trainer how this was possible. He said while they are very young and weak, an elephant is tied by a heavy chain to an immovable iron stake. No matter how hard he tries, he cannot break the chain nor move the stake. Then, no matter how large the elephant becomes, he continues to believe he cannot move as long as he can see the stake in the ground beside him. Many intelligent adult humans are like this circus elephant. They are held back by their own self-imposed limitations which hinders their chance for success and happiness.

Don't be held back by the chain tied to the stake in the ground - snip the chains of your mind and experience the unlimited potential of your abilities.

Dale Brown

THE **POWER** OF
MENTAL IMAGERY

What the mind can believe, so can it achieve.

Marcus Aurelius

It is said that the will to win is not nearly as important as the will to prepare to win. The key to that preparation is done in our minds through mental imagery. That means focusing your mind on an event or circumstance before it happens and playing the desired result of that event over and over again. It doesn't matter if you are an athlete before a big game, a student on the eve of finals, or a businessman preparing for that big presentation. Mental imagery can provide you with the stimulus to provide you with that added edge to win.

Mental imagery has been used by athletes for years with a great degree of success. Take for instance Jean Claude Killy, the famous skier who suffered an injury as was unable to practice for the Olympics. He was the only member of competition that could not physically practice. So, instead he obtained films of the slalom course and watched the videos over and over as he visualized himself racing the slopes. That mental imagery must have provided the practice he needed, because six weeks later, Killy won the gold medal.

Or take the world renowned marksman, Robert Foster. He was out of competition for over a year but returned to break his own world record. How did he do it? He mentally practiced his marksmanship for 10 minutes each day until he was ready once again for competition.

Bruce Jenner also credits mental imagery for each event in the decathlon in the 1976 Olympics in which he captured the Gold Medal in world record setting fashion.

Former great Bill Russell of the Boston Celtics studied every opponent so closely that he could actually play "movies" of them in his mind and therefore they would not be able to surprise him in the game.

But mental imagery isn't just for athletes. It can work for you in your daily life. You have a big sales presentation to make to clients. Instead, of worrying about the result, start thinking the result in your mind. When the times comes for the presentation, you will be prepared because you have practiced the scenario over a hundred times and you may even surprise yourself with the actual results.

It has been said that people tend to live up to their own images of themselves. Take some time out today and put positive mental imagery to work for you.

F.E.A.R.
False Evidence Appearing Real

How often do we let our fears interrupt our plans and goals for success?

There is not a better way of overcoming fear than by taking the word fear itself and breaking it down by its letters F.E.A.R. which actually stand for False Evidence Appearing Real. And when you think of Fear in this context, it becomes easier to overcome it.

Bill Emmerton was a man who overcame fear in a big way.

Bill, in his late 40's, had set a goal of running through Death Valley. Most people already knew about the torturing heat of the Death Valley desert, but most didn't know that this vast hot bed is over 125 miles long.

As Bill began his journey the temperature was 106 blistering degrees and soon was met head-on by a raging wind-sand storm. The storm was so severe that it picked Bill up off the ground and blew him 15 feet. But Bill refused to let fear stop him. He simply dusted himself off and got up and continued his journey.

Later in the run, he was overcome from sulfur fumes. His wife, following in a camper, soaked his clothes in water, massaged his legs, and three minutes later he was back on the road.

By now. the temperature had escalated to 135 degrees and Bill actually had to finish with the toe of his shoe cut off to allow for the flow of blood. But the key thought in the sentence is that he did indeed finish.

Bill didn't let the fear of heat, or of the desert, or of pain interfere with his final goal, finishing the run. You see, Bill demonstrated through his actions that fear was simply False Evidence Appearing Real.

The fear of failure will never overtake you, if your determination to succeed is strong enough.

THE BEAR AND TWO TRAVELERS

A Loyal friend comes in when the whole world goes out.

Once there were two men traveling together when suddenly they spied a bear. Before the bear saw them, one of the men ran to a tree by the side of the road and climbed up into its branches and hid. The other man was not nearly as nimble as his companion. He could not escape and his only chance was to throw himself to the ground and pretend to be dead.

The bear came up and sniffed all around the fellow. The man laid there motionless while holding his breath. Until finally, after what seemed like an eternity, the bear went away.

After he had gone, the traveler in the tree came down and asked what it was the bear had whispered to him when he put his mouth to his ear.

The second man replied, "He told me to never travel with a friend who will leave at the first sign of danger."

LOYALTY
TOP TO BOTTOM

There can be no success in any organization whether it be a basketball team, a business or especially a family, if there is no unconditional loyalty. Loyalty must come from all levels in order to reach every level.

Some 2,500 year ago, a great Chinese leader named Sun Tzu chronicled his leadership philosophy In the book the "Art of War". In it he wrote, "If you regard your soldiers as your children they will follow you into the deepest valleys; look on them as your own beloved sons, and they will stand by you even unto death."

An example of this, is the story of General Wu Chi. Known for wearing the same clothes and eating the same rations of that of the common soldiers, he was renowned for sharing every hardship with his men. On one occasion, one of his soldiers was suffering from an abscess, and it was Wu Chi himself who sucked out the virus. The soldier's mother hearing this began wailing. When asked why she would cry over such a thing, the woman replied: "Many years ago, Lord Wu performed a similar service for my husband, who never left him afterward. And now he has done the same for my son Because of the generals loyalty, so too will my husband and son pledge their undying loyalty to the leader and his cause."

While an extreme example, this story of war, soldiers and leaders does pertain to us all. An ounce of loyalty is worth a pound of cleverness. Without loyalty you have no cause with which to work and fight for. Loyalty is faithful to the cause or ideal. It creates a bond that nothing or no one can break.

Success is getting up one more time than you fall.

"Fight one more round. When your feet are so tired that you have to shuffle back to the center of the ring, fight one more round. When your arms are so tired that you can hardly lift your hands to come on guard, fight one more round. When your nose is bleeding, and your eyes are swollen and you are so tired that you wish your opponent would crack you in the jaw and put you to sleep, fight one more round - remembering that the man who always fights one more round is never whipped."

Former Heavyweight Boxing Champion of the World,
James "Gentleman Jim" Corbett

THE
TWO HEADED
SNAKE

It is amazing what can be accomplished if nobody cares who gets the credit.

A rare two headed snake had been discovered and captured and was being studied by researchers at the University of Tennessee in Knoxville. When the researchers would feed the snake a mouse, one head would get a grip on one end of the rodent while the second head would get a grip on the other end. In a stalemate tug-of-war, neither head captured the prize. But perhaps the most interesting part of the story was that the snake would eventually die if the researchers couldn't do something to stop the two heads from fighting for the food. The moral; the two mouths were feeding the same stomach, but the stomach was not getting fed because the two heads were fighting against each other.

Unbelievably, there are some teams, businesses and even families very much like the two-headed snake.

Peter Morin, once said "The world would be better off if people tried to become better. And people would become better if they stopped trying to become better off. For when everybody tries to become better off, nobody is better off. But when everybody tries to become better, everybody becomes better off."

The best potential of "ME" is "WE."

GOAL
DEVELOPMENT

Before you can score, you must have a goal.

Being the very best you can be is a never-ending job. Just because you were the best you could be yesterday, doesn't mean you can take a day off today. You must constantly work at improving yourself by not only thinking positive but by setting goals for yourself. If you don't have a goal then you'll never know which direction you're heading.

Therefore, the first and most important phase in goal development is to have one. Decide what it is exactly you want to accomplish. In a speech given by Dr. Benjamin Mayers, the President Emeritus at Morehouse college he summarized goal development when he said:

"...It must be born in mind that the tragedy in life doesn't lie in not reaching your goal– the tragedy lies in having no goal to reach... It isn't a calamity to die with dreams unfulfilled– but it is a calamity not to dream... it is not a disaster to be unable to capture your ideal– but it is a disaster to have no ideal to capture... It is not a disgrace not to reach the stars– But it is a disgrace to have no stars to reach for... not failure, but low aim is sin."

After you decide what your short term and long term goals are– the next step is to write them down. Unless you actually write them down on a piece of paper, they will remain abstract ideas or dreams. By writing your goals down - you set your plan in motion. Begin with your short term goals building up to your long term goals and dreams.

For example, if your long term goal is to become a marathon runner, you can't begin with the Boston Marathon, you have to steadily work to the goal by first making a commitment to run each day. Then you start by running around the block. The next week run around the block twice Then run around the neighborhood, then down the road, until you are running 30 miles each day and now you fly to New York.

You see. the long term goal may seem impossible at first, but as you begin to accomplish your smaller goals the larger ones won't seem so impossible.

Goals setting provides you with the power to accomplish the impossible!

DON'T QUIT

When things go wrong, as they sometimes will,
When the road you're trudging seems all uphill,
When the funds are low and the debts are high,
And you want to smile, but you have to sigh,
When care is pressing you down a bit,
Rest, if you must — but don't you quit

Life is queer with its twists and turns,
As everyone of us sometimes learns,
And many a failure turns about,
When he might have won had he stuck it out;
Don't give up, though the pace seems slow—
You might succeed with another blow.

Often the goal is nearer than,
It seems to a faint and faltering man,
Often the struggler has given up,
When he might have captured the victor's cup,
And he learned too late, when night slipped down,
How close he was to the golden crown.

Success is failure turned inside out,
The silver tint to the clouds of doubt—
And you never can tell how close you are,
It may be near when it seems afar;
So stick to the fight when you're hardest hit-
It's when things seem worst that you mustn't quit.

Author Unknown

The enemy I had, I didn't even know.
He followed me unseen, wherever I would go.

He blocked my plans, he blocked my way,
He countered me, even before I could say.

Each time I would make the effort to try,
He made me afraid, so I'd let things pass by.

One night I caught him and grabbed for his mask;
I wanted to see, I wanted to ask.

But to my amazement as I looked at his face,
It was me that I saw, and I prayed for GOD'S GRACE.

The enemy who had been hiding inside,
I finally let go of, and the enemy died.

My new friend inside shares an exciting new way:
He says "YES WE CAN" as we start out each day.

Our SPIRIT in life is the KEY TO IT ALL.
Our BELIEF deep inside picks us up when we fall.

I can run LIFE'S RACE with a CALM INNER PEACE.
I GO FOR IT NOW WITH TOTAL RELEASE.

Author Unknown

The Race

*D*efeat! He lay there silently, a tear dropped from his eye.
"There s no sense running anymore - three strikes, I'm out - why try?"
The will to rise had disappeared, all hope had fled away.
So far behind, so error prone, closer all the way.
"I've lost, so what's the use, he thought. I'll live with my disgrace."
But then he thought about his dad who soon he d have to face.
"Get up," an echo sounded low. Get up and take your place.
You were not meant for failure here, so get up and win the race"

*W*ith borrowed will. "Get up," It said, "You haven't lost at all,
For winning is not more than this - to rise each time you fall."
So up he rose to win once more, and with a new commit,
He resolved that win or lose, at least he wouldn't quit.
So far behind the others now, the most he'd ever been,
Still he gave it all he had and ran as though to win.
Three times he'd fallen stumbling, three times he rose again,
Too far behind to hope to win, he'd still run to the end.

*T*hey cheered the winning runner as he crossed, first place,
Head high and proud and happy; no falling, no disgrace.
But when the fallen youngster crossed the line, last place,
The crowd gave him the greater cheer for finishing the race.
And even though he came in last, with head bowed low unproud;
You would have thought he won the race, to listen to the crowd.
And to his dad he sadly said, I didn't do so well."
To me, you won, his father said. You rose each time you fell"

*A*nd now when things seem dark and hard and difficult to face,
The memory of that little boy helps me in my race.
For all of life is like that race, with ups and downs and all,
And all you have to do to win - is rise each time you fall.
"Quit! Give up, you re beaten," they still shout in my face.
But another voice within me says, "Get up and win that race."

Author Unknown

What's a Friend?

What is a friend? I will tell you. It is a person with whom you dare to be yourself. Your soul can be naked with him. He seems to ask of you to put on nothing, only to be what you are. He does not want you to be better or worse. When you are with him, you feel as a prisoner feels who has been declared innocent. You do not have to be on your guard. You can say what you think, so long as it is genuinely you. He understands those contradictions in your nature that lead others to misjudge you. With him you breathe freely. You can avow your little vanities and envies and hates and vicious sparks, your meanness and absurdities and, in opening them up to him, they are lost, dissolved on the white ocean of his loyalty. He understands. You do not have to be careful. You can abuse him, neglect him, tolerate him. Best of all, you can keep still with him. It makes no matter. He likes you— he is like fire that purges to the one. He understands. You can weep with him, sin with him, laugh with him. pray with him. Through it all and underneath— he sees, knows and loves you. A friend? What is a friend? Just one, I repeat, with whom you dare to be yourself.

C. Raymond Beran

Don't Be  to Take a Risk

To *Laugh* is to risk appearing the fool,

To *Weep* is to risk appearing sentimental,

To *Reach Out For Another* is to risk involvement.

To *Expose Feelings* is to risk exposing your true-self,

To *Place your ideas, your dreams before the crowd*, is to risk their loss,

To *Love* is to risk not being loved in return.

To *Live* is to risk dying,

To *Hope* is to risk despair,

To *Try* is to risk failure,

But risks must he taken

Because the greatest hazard in life is to risk nothing.

The person who risks nothing does nothing, has nothing, is nothing.

He may avoid suffering and sorrow - but he simply cannot learn,

feel, change, grow, love... live

Chained by his certitudes, he is a slave.

He has forfeited freedom

Only a person who risks is free.

By Carol Sapin Gold

Be Honest ← → *with Yourself*

*E*very person should be his own hard taskmaster. We are all builders of "alibis" and creators of "excuses" in support of our shortcomings. We are not seeking facts and truths as they are, but as we wish them to be.

We prefer words of flattery to those of cold, unbiased truth, wherein lies the weakest spot of man. Furthermore, we are up in arms against those who dare to uncover the truth for our benefit.

We go through life stumbling and falling and struggling to our knees, and struggling and falling some more, making asses of ourselves and going down, finally in defeat, largely because we either neglect or flatly refuse to learn the truth about ourselves.

By Napoleon Hill

IT CAN BE DONE

True cowardice is marked by chronic skepticism,
which always says,"It can't be done."

The man who misses all the fun; Is he who says, "It can't be done."

In solemn pride he stands aloof; and greets each venture with reproof.

Had he the power he'd efface; The history of the human race;

We'd have no radio or motor cars,; No streets lit by electric stars;

No telegraph nor telephone,; We'd linger in the age of stone.

The world would sleep if the things were run; By men who say,
"It Can't be done."

Author Unknown

Never Give Up

No one I know has ever experienced one success after another without defeats, failures, disappointments, and frustrations galore along the way. Learning to overcome these times of agony is what separates the winners from the losers.

The biggest difference between people who succeed at any difficult endeavor and those who do not is not usually talent. It tends to be persistence.

Who needs rejection? Who wants to face failure? Who enjoys criticism? Who wants to run the risk of getting knocked down again and again? It takes more self-esteem than lots of people can muster. But it's often been said about highly successful people that they are just individuals who got up one more time than they fell down. If we feel good about ourselves, we don't feel so bad about difficulties that fall across our paths. We're not embarrassed to take a fall and pick ourselves back up. And if we come to understand the true nature of a successful life as a journey, during which many obstacles will need to be faced and overcome, we can develop a new and more positive attitude about the determined persistence we need to succeed.

Always remember, nothing is as good as it seems or as bad as it seems
and Confucius wisely stated "the gem cannot be polished without
friction, nor man perfected without trials."

Tom Morris

To: Jesus, Son of Joseph
Woodcrafter's Carpenter Shop
Nazareth 25922

From: Jordan Management Consultants

Dear Sir:

Thank you for submitting the resumes of the twelve men you have picked for managerial positions in your new organization. All of them have not taken our battery of tests; and we have not only run the results through the computer, but also arranged personal interviews for each of them with our psychologist and vocational aptitude consultant.

The profiles of all tests are Included, and you will want to study each of them carefully.

As a part of our service, we make some general comments for your guidance, much as an auditor will include some general statements. This is given as a result of staff consultation, and comes without any additional fee.

It is the staff opinion that most of your nominees are lacking background, education and vocational aptitude for the type of enterprise you are undertaking. They do not have the team concept. We would recommend that you continue your search for persons of experience in managerial ability and proven capability.

Simon Peter is emotionally unstable and given to fits of temper. Andrew has absolutely no qualities of leadership. The two brothers, James and John, the sons of Zebedee, place personal interest above company loyalty. Thomas demonstrates a questioning attitude that would tend to undermine morale. We feel that it is our duty to tell you that Matthew has been blacklisted by the Greater Jerusalem Better Business Bureau; James, the son of Alphaeus, and Thaddaaeus definitely have radical leanings, and they both registered a high score on the manic-depressive scale.

One of the candidates, however, shows great potential. He is a man of ability and resourcefulness, meets people well, has a keen business mind, and has contacts in high places. He is highly motivated, ambitious, and responsible. We recommend Judas Iscariot as your controller and right-hand man. All of the other profiles are self-explanatory.

We wish you every success in your new venture.

Sincerely yours,

Jordan Management Consultants

THIS
REQUEST

The thought occurred to me the other day,
that I am stuck with myself in every way.

No matter how much blame or credit to others that I try to give,
it's really up to me - the type of life I shall live.

I, for one, don't want to stand at the setting sun,
and hate myself for the things left undone.

But most of all - now - in the present,
with undetermined time to go, I want to learn,
what all wise men already know

That I can never hide myself from me,
For I see what others may never see.

So good Lord, I make this request.

Help me to improve my life,
and never be satisfied with less than my best.

Author Unknown

THE C's OF SUCCESS

1 We need a clear conception of what we want, a vivid vision, a goal or set of goals powerfully imagined.

2 We need a strong confidence that we can attain our goals.

3 We need a focused concentration on what it takes to reach our goal.

4 We need a stubborn consistency in pursuing our vision, a determined persistence in thought and action.

5 We need an emotional commitment to the importance of what we're doing, and to the people with whom we're doing it.

6 We need a good character to guide us and keep us on a proper cause.

7 We need a capacity to enjoy the process along the way.

Author Unknown

Famous

Do you sometimes think you are a failure? Consider failures of some of the most brilliant contributors to our heritage.

Sir Winston Churchill (1874-1965), British Statesman
Churchill's father considered his son so dull that he doubted whether he could ever earn a living. Churchill failed the entrance exams to Sandhurst twice and was taken out of Harrow so that he could study with a "crammer" (tutor).

Giacomo Puccini (1858-1924), Italian Opera Composer
Puccini's first music teacher gave up on teaching him music because he had "no talent."

Albert Einstein (1879-1955) German Physicist
Einstein spoke haltingly until he was nine and after that responded to questions only after much deliberation. His poor performance in all classes except math prompted a teacher to ask him to drop out of school, telling Einstein he'd never amount to anything. Einstein failed his first entrance exam at Zurich's Polytechnic Institute.

Charles Darwin (1809-1882) English Naturalist
Darwin's father once told him: "you care for nothing but shooting, dogs, and rat-catching, and you will be a disgrace to yourself and all of your family. Darwin failed dismally in a medical course at Edinborough University and scraped through many of his courses at Cambridge.

Sir Isaac Newton (1642-1727), English Scientist
Newton was allowed to get an education only because he proved to be a complete failure in running his family's farm. He started out in the lowest form of his school.

Pablo Picasso (1881-197) Spanish Painter
Picasso could barely read or write at age 10 and he was considered a "hopeless pupil" because he refused to learn mathematics.

Thomas Edison (1847-1931) U. S inventor
Edison's teachers described him as "addled," his father thought he was a "dunce", and his headmaster warned that Edison "would never make a success of anything."

Author Unknown

THE Art of Living

Brian Cavanaugh

The art of living is rooted in learning to recognize a critical principle:

What's Important Now!!

Now is the key concept in this principle for living;.For Now is the only time-frame in which we live and work, sleep and play. Life, you see, is but a continuous progression of "NOW" moments.

By doing NOW what is important- whatever that might be in each person's own, unique life- as a student, parent, a coach, a teacher, in work, or in relationships- is to ascend the pinnacle of living.

Yet, in life, winning, itself, should not be our main goal. Winning, actually is a by-product in a succession of NOW'S.

Winning in life is a process of focusing on the- "NOW" moment and of recognizing what is important, at this moment. When this process is in right order is when we will have won. Usually, in this process, however, we are too swept up in the present moment to realize if we are winning, or not. Looming before us, there is only this Now.

So. when this concept NOW becomes your fixed intention; when you do what is important, then you will have won. For NOW spelled backwards is WON. And so it is in the art of living- WHAT 'S IMPORTANT NOW!

Live NOW, and you will have WON!

PLAY THE GAME MY SON

This is your first game, son I hope that you win. I hope that you win for your sake, not mine. It's a good feeling. Like the whole world is yours, But it passes, this feeling. And what lasts is what you've learned. And what you learn about is life. That's what sports is all about. Life. The whole thing is played Out in an afternoon. The happiness of life. The miseries, The joys. The heartbreaks. There's no telling what will turn up. There's no telling whether they'll toss you out in the first five minutes or whether you'll you'll stay for the long haul. There's no telling how you'll do. You might be a hero or you might be absolutely nothing. There's just no telling. Too much depends on chance. On how the ball bounces. I'm not talking about the game, son. ...I'm talking about life. but it's life that the game is all about. just as I said. Because every good game is life. And life is a game, A Serious one. Dead serious. But that's what you do with serious things. You do your best. You take what comes. You take what comes. And you run with it. Winning is fun. Sure. But winning is not the point, Wanting to win is the point. Not giving up is the point Never being satisfied with what you've done is the point. Play to win. Sure. But lose like a champion. Because it's not winning that counts.

What counts is trying.

Author Unknown

Life *Enhancers*

"There are three kinds of people in the world today. There are 'well-poisoners', who discourage you and stomp on your creativity and tell you what you can't do. There are 'Lawn-mowers,' people who are well-intentioned but self-absorbed, they tend to their own needs, mow their own lawns and never leave their yards to help another person. Finally, there are 'Life-enhancers' people who reach out to enrich the lives or others, to lift them up and inspire them. We need to be life-enhancers, and we need to surround ourselves with Life-enhancers."

Walt Disney

OUR HEROES

Seeing what is right and doing it with firm resolve, despite the opinions of the crowd, is the mark of moral courage.

Here's a hand to the boy who has courage
To do what he knows to be right.
When he fails in the way of temptation,
He has a hard battle to fight.
Who strives against self and his comrades
Will find a most powerful foe.
All honor to him if he conquers.
A cheer for the boy who says, "NO!"
There's many a battle fought daily
The world knows nothing about,
There's many a brave Little soldier
Whose strength puts a legion to rout.
And he who fights sin single-handed

Is more of a hero I say
Than he who leads soldiers to battle
And conquers by arms in the fray.
Be steadfast, my boy, when you're tempted,
To do what you know to be right.
Stand firm by the colors of manhood,
And you will o'ercome in the fight.
"The right," be your battle cry ever
In waging the warfare of life,
And God, who knows who are the heroes,
Will give you the strength for the strife.

Phoebe Cary

AROUND THE YEAR
with
Emmet Fox
A Book of Daily Readings

There exists a mystic Power that is able to transform your life so thoroughly, so radically, so completely, that when the process Is completed your own friends would hardly recognize you, and in fact, you would scarcely be able to recognize yourself.

It can lift you out of an invalid's bed, and free you to go out into the world to shape your life as you will. It can throw open the prison door and liberate the captive.
This Power can do for you that which is probably that most Important thing of all in your present stage: It can find your true place in life for you, and put you into it.

But where is this wonderful Power to be contacted?

The answer is simple- this Power is to be found within your own consciousness, the last place that most people would look for it. Within your own mentality there lies a source of energy stronger than electricity, more potent than high explosives, unlimited and inexhaustible. You only need to make conscious contact with it to set it working.

Once you have contacted the Power within, and have allowed it to take over your responsibilities for you, it will direct and govern all your affairs from the greatest to the least.

Be True to Yourself

I have to live with myself and so I want to be fit for myself to know.
I want to be able to, as the days go by, always to look myself straight in the eye.
I don't want to have to stand with the setting sun and hate myself for the things I've done
I want to be able to go out with my head erect.
I want to be able to deserve all people's respect.
For here In this struggle for fame and self, I want to be able to like myself.
I don't want to have to look at myself and know that I'm bluster and bluff, an empty show
I know what others may never know.
I see what others may never see and so I want to be self-respecting and conscious free.

Author Unknown

---

*T*he turning point at which you begin to attain success is usually defined by some form of defeat or failure. With this realization, you need not accept defeat as failure but only as a temporary event that may prove to be a blessing in disguise.

No one who has attained success has not met with some form of failure comparable with the scope of his or her success. Edison "failed" with more than ten thousand different attempts to create a light bulb before he hit on the formula that worked. Jonas Salk tried countless different media to cultivate the polio virus for a vaccine before he discovered that monkey brain tissue did the job. Defeat, however, does not promise the full blown flower of benefit, only the seed from which some benefit may be coaxed. You must recognize the seed, nurture, and cultivate it by definiteness of purpose; otherwise it will never sprout. Time is relentless in preserving the seed of an equivalent benefit that hides within a defeat. The best time to begin looking for that seed in a new defeat is now. But you can also examine past losses for the seeds they contain. Indeed, sometimes the weight of the loss prevents you from searching at the time. But now, with your increased wisdom and experience, you are ready to examine any loss for the lesson it can teach

Learn From Adversity and Defeat
by Napoleon Hill

you. If you accept defeat as an inspiration to try again with renewed confidence and determination, attaining success will be only a matter of time. The secret to this i your positive mental attitude. Remember, positive mental attitude attracts success You need that attraction most when coping with defeat, Redouble your efforts to maintain and build your PMA when adversity strikes, and use your applied faith in yourself and your purpose to put you PMA into action. That is the fundamental lesson in learning from adversity and defeat.

Our strength grows out of our weakness. Not until we are pricked and stung and sorely shot at, awakens the indignation which arm itself with secret forces. A great man is alway willing to be little. While he sits on the cushion of advantages he goes to sleep. When he is pushed, tormented defeated, he has a chance to learn something, he has been put on his wits on his manhood; he has gained facts learned from his ignorance; been cured of the insanity of conceit; has go moderation and real skill

Ralph Waldo Emerson

Live LIFE

Think freely. Practice patience. Smile often. Savor special moments. Live God's message, Make new friends, Rediscover old ones, Tell those you love that you do. Feel deeply, Forget trouble. Forgive an enemy. Hope. Grow. Be crazy. Count your blessings. Observe miracles. Make them happen. Discard worry. Give. Give in. Trust enough to take. Pick some flowers. Share them. Keep a promise, Look for rainbows. Gaze at stars. See beauty everywhere. Work hard. Be wise. Try to understand. Take time for people. Make time for yourself. Laugh heartily. .Spread joy, Take a chance. Reach out. Let someone in. Try something new. Slowdown. Be soft sometimes. Believe in yourself. Trust others. See a sunrise. Listen to rain. Trust life. Have faith. Enjoy wonder. Comfort a friend. Have good ideas. Make some mistakes. Learn from them. Celebrate Life.

Author Unknown

The Bike Ride

Life is like riding a bicycle. You don't fall off until you stop pedaling.
Claude Pepper, U.S. Congressman

At first I saw God as an observer, like my judge, keeping track of things I did wrong. This way. God would know whether I merited heaven or hell when I died. He was always out there, sort of like the President. I recognized His picture when I saw it, but I didn't really know Him at all.

But later on, when i recognized my higher power better, it seemed as though life was rather like a bike ride on a tandem bike, and I noticed God was in the back helping me pedal.

I don't know when it was that He suggested we change places, but life has not been the same since...

When I had control, I thought I knew the way. It was always the shortest distance between two points.

But when He took the lead. He knew delightful cuts, up mountains, and through rocky places and at breakneck speeds; it was all I could do to hang on! Even though it looked like madness. He kept saying, "Pedal, pedal!"

I worried and became anxious, asking. "Where are you taking me?" He just laughed and didn't answer, and I found myself starting to trust when I'd say, "I'm scared," He would lean back and touch my hand.

I did not trust him at first, in control of my life. I thought He'd wreck it. But He knew bike secrets, knew how to make it bend to take sharp corners, jump to clear places filled with rocks, fly to shorten scary passages.

And I'm learning to shut up and pedal in the strangest places, and I'm beginning to enjoy the view and the cool breeze on my face with my delightful constant companion, my God. And when I'm sure I can't go on anymore He just smiles and says, *"Pedal..."*

Author Unknown

You You You You

YOU are the fellow that has to decide
Whether to do it or toss it aside,
You are the fellow who makes up your mind,
Whether you'll lead or linger behind,
Whether you'll try for the goal that's afar,
Or just be contended to stay where you are,
Take it or leave it, here's something to do,
Just think it over- It's all up to you.
What do you wish? To be known as a shirk,
Or known as a good man who's willing to work.,
Scorned as a loafer, or praised by your chief,
Rich man or poor man or beggar or thief,
Eager or earnest or dull through the day,
Honest or crooked. It's you that must say,
You must decide in the face of the test,
Whether you'll shrink or give it your best!!!

Author Unknown

The Things That Haven't Been Done Before

Edgar Guest

The ones who dared to do what we now take for granted are the ones we remember.

The things that haven't been done before,
Those are the things to try;
Columbus dreamed of an unknown shore
At the rim of the far-flung sky,
And his heart was bold and his faith was strong
As he ventured in dangers new,
And he paid no heed to the jeering throng
Or the fears of the doubting crew.

The many will follow the beaten track
With guideposts on the way.
They live and have lived for ages back
With a chart for every day.
Someone has told them it's safe to go
On the road he had traveled o'er,
And all that they ever strive to know
Are the things that were known before.

A few strike out, without map or chart,
Where never a man has been,
From the beaten paths they draw apart
To see what not man has seen.
There are deeds they hunger alone to do;
Though battered and bruised and sore,
They blaze the path for the many, who
Do nothing not done before.

The things that haven't been done before
Are the tasks worthwhile today;
Are you one of the flock that follows, or
Are you one that shall lead the way?
Are you one of the timid souls that quail
At the jeers of a doubting crew,
Or dare you, whether you win or fail,
Strike out for a goal that's new?

While Daring Greatly

*I*t is not the critic who counts; not the man who points out how the strong man stumbled, or where the doer of deeds could have done them better. The credit belongs to the man who is actually in the arena, whose face is marred by dust and sweat and blood, who strives valiantly, who errs and comes short again and again, who knows the great enthusiasms, the great devotions, who spends himself in a worthy cause, who at the best knows in the end the triumph of high achievement, and who, at the worst, if he fails, at least fails while daring greatly, so that his place will never be with those timid souls who know neither victory nor defeat.

Theodore Roosevelt

The Bridge Builder

An old man going a lone highway
Came in the evening cold and gray
To a chasm vast and deep and wide.
The old man crossed in the twilight dim,
The sullen stream had no fears for him.
But he stopped when safe on the other side
and built a bridge to span the tide

"Old man." said a fellow pilgrim near,
"You are wasting your strength with building here
Your journey will end with the ending day
You never again will pass this way
You've crossed the chasm deep and wide,
Why build you this bridge at evening tide?

The builder lifted his old gray head
"Good friend, in the path I have come", he said
"There followeth after me today
A youth whose feet must pass this way.
This chasm which has been as naught to me
To that fair-haired youth might a pitfall be,
He, too, must cross in the twilight dim,
Good friend, I am building the bridge for him."

Will Alton Dromgoole

HOW To FAIL In Everything

✓ Knock everything systematically. No matter what you hear, expect the worst. This will build an inferiority complex in yourself that will inevitably destroy any good thing in your life.

✓ Mind everyone else's business. This will ensure you neglecting your own.

✓ Try to please everyone and take everyone's advice. This will leave your mind in complete chaos.

✓ Try to live on bluff. You are certain to be found out before long, and them no one will respect you again

✓ Believe everything you hear. Someone said it, so, of course, it must be true.

✓ Never perform today what you can possibly postpone until tomorrow.

✓ Have no organized arrangements. Trust luck for everything.

✓ Avoid notebooks and rely on memory.

✓ Never be original. Find out what is usually done and copy that.

✓ Realize that you have nothing more to learn. This will destroy all danger of success.

✓ Give yourself airs and high-hat everybody. This will make you universally unpopular.

✓ Sneer at those who are more successful than yourself. This will have a particularly damaging effect on your own life.

✓ Tell yourself that it is now too late and that you really did not have the proper equipment. It will be especially helpful to keep saying that people are against you.

✓ Never learn from experience. Keep on doing the same darn fool things time after time.

✓ Never wait to hear the other side of the story. Knowing both sides will only unsettle your mind.

✓ Use your wit destructively. Be smart at the expense of absent people. This is sure to be carried to them and will make enemies for you.

✓ Stand on your dignity. Never forget that you have a position to keep up, even if you have nothing to keep it up on. Never do any work that is not just to your liking. This policy should bring you safely into the bread line.

✓ Try to get everything on the cheap. Beat down everyone. Study and practice to become the perfect "Chiseler." This will build an invincible poverty complex.

✓ Be a sanctimonious humbug, and when you bungle up things, say it is "the Lord's will" or that the trouble Is that you are too good for your surroundings.

✓ Sit down and wait for something to turn up. This is the sovereign recipe for failure.

✓ Finally, conduct your life In all respects as If there were no God.

Author Unknown

Always a Way •

There is always a way to rise, my lad,
always a way to advance,
but the road that leads to Mount Success,
does not pass by the way of chance;

It goes through the stations of work and strive,
through the valley of persevere;
and the man that succeeds while others fail,
must be willing to pay most dear.

For there's always a way to slide:
and the men you find at the foot of the hill,
all sought for an easy ride.

And so on and up,
though the road be rough,
and the storms come thick and fast;

There is room at the top
for the fellow who tries,
and victory comes at last.

Author Unknown

The Dream and the Dreamer

A wild inventor and drifter witnesses the deaths of a number of children drinking contaminated milk. He dreams of finding a way to preserve milk.
Gail Borden
Bordens Milk & Ice Cream

A widower with a young son loses his job at a department store. He dreams of being his own boss and scrapes together $1,500 to open his own store.
George Kinney
Kinney Shoes

Two tinkerers set up shop in the garage of one of their homes with the dream of being on the leading edge of technology. One of their first inventions is an electric harmonica tuner.
William Hewlett & David Packard
Hewlett-Packard Informational Systems

When his older brother was shot down and killed in WW II, this teenager listened to the radio to ease his loneliness and dreamed of someday being an announcer on his own show.
Dick Clark
American Bandstand

Two brothers-in-law with a simple dream of starting a business together and making $75 a week. They have a brilliantly simple marketing philosophy: One product served 31 different ways
Burton Baskin & Irvine Robbins
Baskin & Robins Ice Cream

A 6 year old boy dreamed of a way to make chicken eggs hatch faster. His solution was to sit on the eggs himself. It was the first glimmer of his genius and the start of ideas that would change the world.
Thomas Alva Edison
Inventor of the light bulb, phonograph player and motion pictures

Growing up, a little girl liked to touch people's faces and comb their hair. She loved helping people make themselves pretty and she dreamed of becoming a skin care specialist while she watched her uncle cook up creams and potions on her mother's gas stove.
Estee Lauder
Estee Lauder Cosmetics

In the 1800's, surgery patients die continuously from infections caused by unsanitary conditions. A young dreamer convinces his brother to work with him to find a way to produce sterile bandages.
Robert, Edward & James Johnson
Johnson & Johnson Products

A general practitioner dreams of performing a surgical procedure thought to be impossible. His goal was to achieve this dream before his rheumatoid arthritis prevented him from operating.
Dr. Christian Barnard
First successful human heart transplant surgeon

What is Virtue?

Fortitude- The strength of mind and courage to persevere in the face of adversity.

Temperance- Self-discipline, the control of all unruly human passions and appetites.

Prudence- Practical wisdom and the ability to make the right choice in specific situations.

Justice- Fairness, honesty, lawfulness and the ability to keep one's promises.

Author Unknown

How to Build Loyalty

Many people reject the old-fashioned belief that we owe loyalty to those who are close to us and helped to make us what we are. They also do not believe we owe loyalty to the nation whose benefits we enjoy. In the short run, this disregard of loyalty hurts some people. In the long run, this attitude hurts everyone.

A one-sided, individualistic approach to life may work as long as things are going well, but it is likely to fail when problems arise. Loyalty builds strong, long-lasting mutual relationships that can help overcome temporary setbacks... it leaves both sides better off in the long term.

Loyalty stands us in good stead when times are tough... but it should be established when things are still going well.

FOUR STEPS TO LOYALTY:

Affirmation. Think about the good things others are doing for you. Show them how much you appreciate them... in both word and deed.

Confrontation. Show them that the relationship is Important to you by pointing out how it can be improved. When you disapprove of your friend's behavior don't be afraid to say so... but always constructively.

Complicity. I use this term, which is translated from the French, to mean the sense that you and your friend(s) are separate from the rest of the world. You possess something nobody else has. Feel very happy about it.

Ritual. Find a way to do things for the special people in your circle.

The toughest challenge of personal loyalty is to Stand by another when the going gets tough. Loyalty becomes important only when we are tempted to "jump ship." Fair-weather loyalty is but convenience. The next time you are tempted to leave, think, this is the time to show my loyalty.

Author Unknown

Before the Rainbow

Chris Neck

Have you ever felt so low,
Like Rock-Bottom was your home.
Your self-esteem had plummeted.
You felt so all alone.

One crisis after another.
Why me- you wanted to shout.
Depression clouded your outlook.
There seemed like no way out.

Then consider this quaint example.
Store it in your mind.
Recall it when necessary.
When happiness is hard to find.

An explorer stumbled across a diamond.
It seemed mediocre to him.
It appeared almost worthless.
It's sparkle- a faint dim.

Then he took a knife and file,
And cut it for some time.

And after many hours,
It suddenly began to shine.

The message in this story,
I hope rings loud and true.
That only through tribulations,
Can emerge the true you.

Difficulties are a part of life;
It's tough to overcome them.
But if you bear down and persevere,
you'll emerge as a brilliant gem.

So as you go through life,
Please remember to recall.
That before the rainbow appears,
There's usually some rainfall.

Like the diamond that is cut,
You'll be one of a kind.
By overcoming obstacles,
The more you will shine.

Live and Learn and Pass It On

- I've learned that if someone says something unkind about me, I must live so that no one will believe it.

- I've learned that every great achievement was once considered impossible.

- I've learned that the great challenge of life is to decide what's impossible and to disregard everything else.

- I've learned that you shouldn't compare yourself to the best others can do, but to the best you can do.

- I've learned that whenever I decide something with kindness. I usually make the right decision

- I've learned that people allow themselves to be only as successful as they think they deserve to be.

- I've learned it's a lot easier to react than it is to think.

- I've learned that anger manages everything poorly.

- I've learned that when bad times come. you can let them make you bitter or use them to make you better.

- I've learned that it's just as important to forget a wrong as it is to remember a kindness.

- I've learned that no one can keep a secret.

- I've learned that I don't make many mistakes with my mouth shut

- I've learned that there's no elevator to success. You have to take the stairs.

- I've learned that although there may be reasons to be cynical, it never helps correct the situation.

- I've learned that you shouldn't fight a battle if there's nothing to win.

- I've learned that how people treat me is more a reflection of how they see themselves than how they see me.

- I've learned that you either control your attitude or it controls you.

- I've learned that success is more often the result of hard work than of talent.

- I've learned that it is impossible to accomplish anything worthwhile without the help of other people.

- I've learned that a good leader accepts bad news calmly.

- I've learned that failures always blame someone else.

- I've learned that the important thing is not what others think of me, but what I think of me.

- I've learned that my worst decisions were made when I was angry.

- I've learned that if you allow someone to make you angry, you have to let him conquer you.

- I've learned that hatred is like acid. It destroys the vessel that holds it.

- I've learned that plotting revenge only allows the people who hurt you to hurt you longer.

- I've learned that regrets over yesterday and the fear of tomorrow are twin thieves that rob us of the moment.

- I've learned that you form a committee to "study the matter" when you really don't want to do anything.

- I've learned to be generous with praise but cautious with promises.

- I've learned that you shouldn't speak unless you can improve on the silence.

Author Unknown

Does It Make Sense?

"I have concluded that the accumulation of wealth, even if I could achieve it, is an insufficient reason for living. When I reach the end of my days, a moment or two from now, I must look backward on something more meaningful than the pursuit of houses and land and machines and stocks and bonds. Nor is the fame of any lasting benefit. I will consider my earthly existence to have been wasted unless I can recall a loving family, a consistent investment in the lives of people, and an earnest attempt to serve the God who made me. Nothing else makes much sense."

By James Dobson, Jr.

You Can DO IT If You DON'T GIVE UP

We would cease to fear or to run away from trying experiences if we observed, from the biographies of men of destiny, that nearly every one of them was sorely tried and run throughout the mill of merciless experience before he "arrived".

Defeat is the plainest and most effective language in the world. When we listen to no other language defeat speaks to us. Defeat talks to us in language all it's own: a language to which we must Listen whether we like it or not.

Who never has suffered, he has lived but half

Who never failed, he never strove or sought,

Who never wept is stranger to a laugh,

And he who never doubted never thought

Life is a cycle of varying events-fortunes and misfortunes. We cannot stop this wheel of fate from turning, but we can modify the misfortune it brings us by remembering that good fortune will follow, just as surely as night follows day, if we keep faith with ourselves and earnestly and honestly do our best.

Napoleon Hill

The happiest people in the world are people who love what they are doing, regardless of whether wealth, fame, power, and elevated social status ever come their way.

The people who attain true success in their lives are people who enjoy a good measure of both fulfillment and happiness as they invest themselves in worthwhile pursuits.

Be The Best You Can Be

"Regret for the things we did can be tempered by time; il is regret for the things we did not do that is inconsolable." Don't miss the opportunity. Don't pass up the chance. Be the best that you can be. Be all you can be. Do the best you can do. Give it everything you've got. Then you can live a life of inner satisfaction, not inconsolable regret.

We set goals, we attain them, and then we ease up. After a big project is completed, after a high goal is reached, we coast. Not just for a day, or a week, but for the long haul. And that's when the competition moves in. This is the human tendency that on a smaller scale allows for dramatic comebacks in sporting events. It's a very dangerous habit.

Everyone deserves a rest after successfully striving for a goal and making it. So take the afternoon off. But don't have an off year.

Too often today's excellence is tomorrow's mediocrity.

Dr. Tom Morris

DALE BROWN

The Power of Setting Goals

One of the greatest tragedies in life is to discover on your deathbed that you've never really lived, that your whole life has bean a futile investment in idle activity.

Statistics show that by the time Americans reach the age of sixty-five, 95 percent of them are either dependent upon friends, relatives, or charity, or they must continue to work. In the richest land of all, many people die poverty-stricken because they never set any goals for their lives- goals that could have included plans to obtain their dreams or simply to ensure a financially secure future.

What separates the average person from the above-average person? The things he or she does with life. What distinguishes the mediocre from the achievers are the goals they set for their lives.

There have been countless people who have been down and out who suddenly became super achievers because they learned to set goals and work toward them. Goals can give a person power then never knew existed because they finally have something to be enthusiastic and excited about.

Following are seven major reasons why people won't set goals. Perhaps you'll find yourself or some of your friends in the following descriptions.

1. WE DON'T KNOW WHAT WE WANT.
Fist of all, the reason most of us never get what we want is because we honestly don't know what we want. The average college student changes his or her major four times before graduation. Ninety-five percent of those who do graduate from college end up in vocations different from those in which they got their degrees.

2. WE DON'T BELIEVE GOALS WORK.
Dr. William James, the father of American psychology, said that your belief at the beginning of any project determines its outcome. If you believe something won't work, you probably won't try it.

3. WE CONFUSE ACTIVITY WITH ACCOMPLISHMENT.
Most of us have been told that we'll get ahead if we'll "work hard." So we work, and work. and work, and nothing happens. We don't achieve those dreams that we've dreamed. People don't get ahead simply by working "hard." They get ahead by working "smart."

4. WE CONFUSE WISHES AND WANTS WITH GOALS.
Most of us have just as many wishes as we have wants. "I wish I could lose weight." "I want to be a better husband." "I wish I looked better." "I want to go back to college, etc. Someone once said, "if wishes were money, beggars would be kings." A wish by itself won't do any good. It may excite you, but it won't motivate you or disturb you to act- a goal will.

5. WE'RE AFRAID WE'LL FAIL.
When it comes to setting goals, people are afraid of two things; First, they're afraid that if they fail they may discover that what they suspect about themselves is true. They don't want to be seen as a failure, so why take the risk? Second, people are afraid to set goals because they're afraid of success itself. Perhaps low self-esteem makes them believe they can't succeed.

6. WE DO THE URGENT AND NOT THE IMPORTANT.
It's Sunday afternoon and the Broncos are playing. And, of course, tomorrow evening "Monday Night Football" is on. Tuesday night is PTA and there is a prayer meeting at church on Wednesday, etc., etc. All these things are important. But most people tend to do the immediate before they'll even sit down and think about the future.

7. WE DON'T UNDERSTAND THE TRUE FUNCTION OF A GOAL.
The true function of a goal is to produce power. Most people would like to have power. But they think that having power comes before setting goals. It's just the opposite. The goals provide the power you need to become all that you can become. They help you envision what you can be and what you can accomplish in your lifetime. A goal is that surge inside that lifts you, pushes you, and forces you to become the kind of person you have the potential of becoming.

The first of a three-part series taken from Lewis Timber-lake's book, *Born To Win*, Tyndale House Publishers, 1986

Vince Lombardi Credo

*L*eaders are made, They are not born; and they are made just like anything else has been made in this country... by Hard Effort. And that's the price that we all have to pay to achieve that goal, or any goal.

*A*nd despite what we say about being born equal, none of us really are born equal, but rather unequal. And yet the talented are no more responsible for their birthright than the underprivileged. And the measure of each should be what each does in a specific situation.

*I*t is becoming increasingly difficult to be tolerant of a society who has sympathy only for the misfits, only for the maladjusted, only for the criminal, only for the loser. Have sympathy for them, help them, but I think it's also time for all of us to stand up and cheer for the doer, the achiever, the one who recognizes a problem and does something about it, the one who looks at something extra to do for his country,

The Winner The Leader!"

No One Is Beat

No one is beat til he quits

No one is through til he stops

No matter how often he drop

A fellow is not down 'til he lies

In the dust and refuses to rise

fate can slam him and bang him around

And batter his frame "til he's sore

But he never can say that he's downed

While he bobs up serenely for more

A fellow's not down 'til he dies

Nor beat 'til no longer he tries.

Edward White II

Options

Life is just a string of options
Of choices we must make,
Different roads to journey down
Directions we can take.

And there is no perfect choice
Or pre-ordained way to go,
We can't control our destinies
Or direct the river's flow.

But we know that joy cannot exist
Without the risk of pain,
For as flowers bloom in sunshine
They would die without the rain.

Life is full of can-nots
But they're balanced by the clouds,
And where there's a chance for evil
There must be a chance for good.

And when we take our options
Whichever path we choose,
For every chance of winning
There must be a chance to lose.

So your life is what you make it
You pick the pattern and the style,
You can drown in tears and sorrow
Or light pathways with a smile.

And we know life won't be easy
From first cry to final breath,
But remember the alternative
The other side of life, is death...

So if you struggle past the hurdles
Accept the failure with the fun,
If at the end, you're smiling friend
You'll have run your race...and won.

Author Unknown

I CAN'T

"Can't" is a favorite word of some children. Here is the case against it.

Can't is the worst word that's written or spoken;
Doing more harm here than slander and lies;
On It is many a strong spirit broken,
And with It many a good purpose dies.
It springs from the lips of the thoughtless each morning,
And It robs us of the courage we need through the day;
It rings in our ears like a timely sent warning,
And laughs when we falter and fall by the way.

Can't is the father of feeble endeavor,
The parent of terror and halfhearted work;
It weakens the efforts of artisans clever,
And makes of the toiler an indolent shirk.
It poisons the soul of the man with a vision,
It stifles in infancy many a plan,
It greets honest toiling with open derision,
And mocks at the hopes and the dreams of a man.

Can't is a word none should speak without blushing;
To utter it should be a symbol of shame.
Ambition and courage, it daily is crushing;
It blights a man's purpose and shortens his aim.
Despite it with all of your hatred of error;

Refuse it the lodgement it seeks in your brain;
Arm against it as a creature of terror,
And all that you dream of,
You someday shall gain.

Can't is the word that is foe to ambition,
An enemy ambushed to shatter your will;
Its prey is forever the man with a mission.

And bows but to courage and patience and skill.
Hate it, with hatred that's deep and undying,
For once it is welcomed twill break any man;
Whatever the goal you are seeking, keep trying
And answer this demon by saying:

"I CAN."

Edgar Guest

It Takes A Man

Pulpit Helps, June 1992

It takes a man to be a father.

- To discipline his child through the inner life of the spirit, rather than by the brute force of his hand;
- To listen and to share his time and energy even when he is weary or busy with his own interests;
- To be sensitive to his child's needs and pain rather than concerned with his own image and ego;
- To be able to admit a mistake or a failure and ask forgiveness and understanding
- To be patient, honest, open, acknowledging his own impatience, prejudices, frustrations, and the anger and pain of knowing he is less than what he wants to be.
- To take a child into his arms with loving embrace when broken relationships need to be healed;
- To love his child's spontaneity, just as he or she is, rather than demand predetermined and patterned responses;
- To celebrate with his child the spirit of God as they together find it in the beauty of dawn, the breeze caressing their faces, the exhilaration of running, the touch of a hand, the quiet glow of shared love;
- To see in the child the man or woman the child will become, and be grateful for the opportunity to share in their life.

Listening Takes More Than Two Good Ears

Most people think they are good listeners. Most people are wrong. Studies have repeatedly shown they really absorb only about 25 to 30% of what they hear. Unfortunately, listening is the one communication skill we have never been taught. Few people have been trained to listen. Education concentrates on reading, writing and proper speaking. Listening is the neglected stepchild. As a result, people develop bad listening habits which prevent their really taking in much of what is said to them.

HERE ARE FIVE SUGGESTIONS TO IMPROVE YOUR LISTENING SKILL.

1. Rephrase your understanding of what you have been told in your own words and, when possible, check with the source.

2. When you disagree with someone, take extra care to get what he or she says right. Then consider whether:

   a. You may be giving some word or phrase a meaning that is different from what the speaker intended.

   b. The speaker may have more or better information than you on some points in the statements.

3. If you find something you are told exciting, watch out for errors of exaggeration in your understanding of it. A classic example is Orson Welles' radio broadcast "The War Of The Worlds." Hundreds of thousands of listeners ignored all the evidence that it was fiction and firmly believed that Mars had invaded us.

4. Watch out for, and control the emotional booby trap. If the listener hears some of his fondly-held beliefs attacked by the speaker, his mind is likely to use its unoccupied time to draw up arguments against the speaker's position. The opposite situation can also produce poor listening. The result can be that any real differences between the speaker's ideas and those of the listener are likely to be overlooked.

5. If you find something you are told boring, watch out for errors of transposition-Boredom can blot out parts of a message, but it is far more dangerous when it disarranges them. A common cause of boredom is the feeling that you are being told something you already know.

One good way to avoid the errors of transposition- and to increase your receptivity to all parts of a message- is to take that feeling of familiarity as a signal that it is time to seek the unfamiliar.

Listen specifically to determine whether there may not be at least one new item or new juxtaposition of old items. At least there may be some difference in phrasing or in tone of voice to give you a lead to something new.

H.C. Cascante

The Golden Eagle

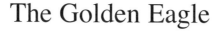

A man found an eagle's egg and put it in the nest of a backyard hen. The eaglet hatched with a brood of chicks and grew up with them.

All his life the eagle did what the backyard chickens did, thinking he was a backyard chicken. He scratched the earth for worms and insects. He clucked and cackled and he would thrash his wings and fly a few feet into the air.

Years passed and the eagle grew very old. One day he saw a magnificent bird far above him in the cloudless sky. It glided in graceful majesty among the powerful wind currents with scarcely a beat of its strong wings. The old eagle looked up in awe. "Who's that?" he asked. "That's the eagle. The king of the birds." said his neighbor "He belongs to the sky. We belong to the earth– we're chickens." So the eagle lived and died a chicken, for that's what he thought he was.

Author Unknown

ENTHUSIASM!

That certain something that makes us great - that pulls us out of the mediocre and commonplace- that builds into us power. It glows and shines- it lights up our faces.

ENTHUSIASM, the keynote that makes us sing and makes men sing with us.

ENTHUSIASM - The maker of friends- the maker of smiles- the producer of confidence. It cries to the world, "*I've got what it takes*." It tells all men that our job is a swell Job- that the house we have is the best house- that company we work for Just suits us- the goods we have are the best.

ENTHUSIASM - The inspiration that makes us '*Wake Up and Live*.' It puts spring into our step- spring into our hearts- a twinkle in our eyes- and gives us confidence in ourselves and our fellow men.

ENTHUSIASM - It changes a dead pan salesman to a producer- a pessimist to an optimist- a loafer to a go-getter.

ENTHUSIASM - If we have it we should thank God for it. If we don't have it, then we should get down on our knees and pray for it.

Upon the plains of hesitation, bleached the bones of countless millions who, on the threshold of victory, sat down to wait, and waiting they died.

Author Unknown

Growth

For every bill I've had to climb
For every that bruised my feet,
For all the blood and sweat and grime
My heart sings but a grateful song
These were things that made me strong

For all the heartaches and the tears
For all the anguish and the pain,
For gloomy days and fruitless years,
and for the hopes that lived in vain,
I do give thanks, for now I know,
These were the things that made me grow!

Tis not the softer things of life,
Which stimulated man's will to strive;

But bleak adversity and strife
Do most to keep man's will alive.
O'er rose-strewn paths the weaklings creep,
But brave hearts dare to climb the steep.

Author Unknown

Maturity

Maturity is the ability to do a job whether you are supervised or not; finish a job once it is started; carry money without spending it, and be able to bear an injustice without wanting to get even.

Maturity is the ability to control anger and settle differences without violence.

Maturity is patience. It is the willingness to postpone immediate gratification in favor of the long-term gain.

Maturity is perseverance, the ability to sweat out a project or a situation in spite of heavy opposition and discouraging setbacks.

Maturity is the capacity to face unpleasantness and frustration, discomfort and defeat without complaint or collapse.

Maturity is humility. It is being big enough to say, "I was wrong." And, when right, the mature person need not experience the satisfaction of saying, "I told you so."

Maturity is the ability to make a decision and stand by it. The immature spend their lives exploring endless possibilities; then they do nothing,

Maturity means dependability, keeping one's word, coming through in a crisis. The immature are masters of The alibi. They are confused and disorganized. Their lives are a maze of broken promises, former friends, unfinished business and good intentions that somehow never materialized.

Maturity is the art of living in peace with that which we cannot change, the courage to change that which can be changed and the wisdom to know the difference!

Author Unknown

IF...

IF I had enough "pull"...
IF I had money...
IF I had a good education...
IF I could get a job...
IF I had good health...
IF I only had time...
IF times were better...
IF other people understood me...
IF conditions around me were only different...
IF I could live my life over again...
IF I did not fear what "they would say"...
IF I had been given a chance...
IF other people didn't "have it in for me"...
IF I could only do what I want...
IF I had been born rich...
IF I could meet "the right people"...
IF I had the talent that some people have...
IF I dared assert myself...
IF people didn't get on my nerves...
IF I could save money...
IF the boss only appreciated me...
IF I only had somebody to help me...
IF my family understood me...
IF I could just get started...
IF I had the personality of some people...
IF my talents were known...
IF I could just get a "break"...
IF I could only get out of debt...
IF I hadn't failed...
IF I knew how...
IF everybody didn't oppose me...
IF I didn't have so many worries...
IF people weren't so dumb...
IF luck were not against me...
IF I were sure of myself...
IF I had not been born under the wrong star...
IF I did not have to work so hard...
IF I didn't have a past...
IF other people would only listen to me...
IF ...and this is the greatest of them all...
IF I had the courage to see myself as I really am, *I would find out what is wrong with me and correct it then I might have a chance to profit by my mistakes and learn something from the experience of others, for I know that there is something wrong with me, or I would now be where I would have been if I had spent more time analyzing my weaknesses, and less time building alibis to cover them.*

Author Unknown

Thought Conditions

♦ Most men fail not because they aim too high, but because they aim at nothing.

♦ Think like people of action; act like people of thought.

♦ The only real limitations we encounter are those which we place on our own minds

♦ Go Into a game believing you are going to do your best- then do it!

♦ The self-motivated man is one who has developed more of the God-given potential all of us possess!

♦ All men are created with an equal opportunity to become unequal!

♦ You are where you are because of the dominating thoughts that occupy your mind!

♦ Do It now! Nothing is successful until it is accomplished.

♦ If a man never fails, it may be because he never tries.

♦ Set your goals high. If you aim for the gutter, that is where you will end up.

♦ Luck is what happens when preparation meets opportunity.

♦ Success is a journey, not a destination.

♦ It's better to get ahead than to get even.

♦ A person who knows, and knows he knows—he is wise. Follow him.

♦ Knowledge makes for confidence.

♦ What is an ideal without life: what is life without an ideal?

Author Unknown

Myself

I have to live with myself, and so
I want to be fit for myself to know,
I want to be able, as days go by,
Always to look myself straight in the eye;
I don't want to stand, with the setting sun,
And hate myself for things I have done.

I don't want to keep on a closet shelf
A lot of secrets about myself,
And fool myself, as I come and go,
Into thinking that nobody else will know
The kind of man I really am;
I don't want to dress up myself in shame.

I want to go out with my head erect
I want to deserve all men's respect;
But here in the struggle for fame and self
I want to be able to like myself.
I don't want to look at myself and know
That I'm bluster and bluff and empty show.

I can never hide myself from me;
I see what others may never see;
I know what others may never know,
I never can fool myself, and so,
Whatever happens, I want to be
Self-respecting and conscience free.

-Edgar A. Guest

Men Who Win

I once knew a man who would figure
    and plan;
The deeds he intended to do,
But when the time came to get into the game;
He never put anything through.

He would dream with a smile of the
    after while;
And the deeds he would do pretty soon,
He was all right at heart, but he would
    never start.
He never could get quite in tune.

If he would have done half the things
    he'd begun;
He'd be listed among those of fame,
But he didn't produce, so he was no use;
Good intentions do not win the game.

It is easy to dream—and to plan and
    to scheme.
And let them drop out of sight;
But the men who put through what their
    dreams bring to view,
Are the men who win out in the fight.

Author Unknown

The Average Man

The world is "NOT" looking for the average man,
One content to live off the fat of the land;
Who like the tree with the one dead limb
Never used the full talents God had given him.

The world is "NOT" looking for the average man
Who is willing to quit just because he can,
And to be satisfied with being better than some,
Not giving a thought about improvement to come.

The world is "NOT" looking for the average man
Who find it an honor with the mediocre to stand,
And finishes the race in the middle of the pack
While the world goes on and never looks back.

The world "IS" looking for the champion man
Who will give his all whenever he can.

And no matter what the cost, he will do his best
Never to be content with being like the rest.

The world "IS" looking for the champion man
Who has the toughness of a calloused hand;
Who is busy at work to improve his skill,
That he might escape being "run-of-the -mill."

The world "IS" looking for the champion man
Who won't say, "I can't " but will say, "I can,"
Who finishes the race in front of the pack,
So intent in his effort he never looks back,

So to you who are preparing for your life's work
Who never intend your job to shirk,
Remember, the champion man could be you,
But only your best will ever do.

Jim Ba

IN EVERY FIELD OF HUMAN ENDEAVOR, HE THAT IS FIRST MUST PERPETUALLY LIVE IN THE WHITE LIGHT OF PUBLICITY, WHETHER THE LEADERSHIP BE VESTED IN A MAN OR IN A MANUFACTURED PRODUCT, EMULATION AND ENVY ARE EVER AT WORK. IN ART - IN LITERATURE - IN MUSIC - IN INDUSTRY - THE REWARD AND THE PUNISHMENT ARE ALWAYS THE SAME. THE REWARD IS WIDESPREAD RECOGNITION, THE PUNISHMENT FIERCE DENIAL AND DETRACTION. WHEN A MAN'S WORK BECOMES A STANDARD FOR THE WHOLE WORLD, IT ALSO BECOMES A TARGET FOR THE SHOTS OF THE ENVIOUS FEW. IF THIS WORK IS MERELY MEDIOCRE, IT WILL BE LEFT SEVERELY ALONE. IF HE ACHIEVES A MASTERPIECE, IT WILL SET A MILLION TONGUES A WAGGING. JEALOUSY DOES NOT PROTRUDE ITS FORKED TONGUE AT THE ARTIST WHO PRODUCES A COMMON PLACE PAINTING. WHATEVER YOU WRITE OR PAINT - OR SING- OR BUILD - NO ONE WILL STRIVE TO SURPASS OR TO SLANDER YOU - UNLESS YOUR WORK BE STAINED WITH THE SEAL OF GENIUS. LONG, LONG AFTER A GREAT WORK OR A GOOD WORK HAS BEEN DONE - THOSE WHO ARE DISAPPOINTED OR ENVIOUS CONTINUE TO CRY OUT THAT IT CANNOT BE DONE. SPITEFUL LITTLE VOICES IN THE DOMAIN OF ART WERE RAISED AGAINST OUR OWN WHISTLER AS A MOUNTEBANK. LONG AFTER THE BIG WORLD HAD ACCLAIMED HIM ITS GREATEST ARTISTIC GENIUS, MULTITUDES FLOCKED TO BAYREUTH TO WORSHIP AT THE MUSICAL SHRINE OF WAGNER WHILE THE LITTLE GROUP OF THOSE WHOM HE HAD DETHRONED AND DISPLACED ARGUED ANGRILY THAT HE WAS NO MUSICIAN AT ALL! THE LITTLE WORLD CONTINUED TO PROTEST THAT FULTON WOULD NEVER BUILD A STEAMBOAT, WHILE THE BIG WORLD FLOCKED TO THE RIVER BANKS TO SEE HIS BOAT STEAM BY! THE LEADER IS ASSAILED BECAUSE HE IS A LEADER AND THE EFFORT TO EQUAL HIM IS MERELY ADDED PROOF OF THAT LEADERSHIP. FAILING TO EQUAL OR TO EXCEL, THE FOLLOWER SEEKS TO DEPRECIATE AND TO DESTROY, BUT ONLY CONFIRMS ONCE MORE THE SUPERIORITY OF THAT WHICH HE STRIVES TO SUPPLANT. THERE IS NOTHING NEW IN THIS. IT IS AS OLD AS THE WORLD AND AS OLD AS THE HUMAN PASSIONS ENVY, FEAR, GREED, AMBITION AND THE DESIRE TO SURPASS. AND IT ALL AVAILS NOTHING. IF THE LEADER TRULY LEADS, HE REMAINS THE LEADER - MASTER POET - MASTER PAINTER - MASTER WORKMAN - EACH IN HIS TURN IS ASSAILED AND EACH HOLDS HIS LAURELS THROUGH THE AGES. THAT WHICH IS GOOD OR GREAT MAKES ITSELF KNOWN - NO MATTER HOW LOUD THE CLAMOR OR DENIAL. THAT WHICH DESERVES TO LIVE- LIVES.

The Penalty of Leadership

This text appeared as an advertisement in the Saturday Evening Post, January 2nd in the year 1915.
copyright Cadillac Motor Car Division.

Keep Climbing

Life is a struggle, a
continual climb,
If we're ever to reach our
goal;
Requiring real effort from
dawn to dusk,
Ere we slip and mar our
soul.
For the road of life is rough
and rugged,
With many a stone in the
way;
And only with courage and a
will to win,
Can we reach the summit one day.
God never intended that the going be
easy,
That our pathway be strewn with flowers;
But by overcoming hardships day by day,
We grow stronger in our various powers.
Then up with your chin and out with a smile,

Start pushing your way to the top;
The higher you climb, the better the view;
Keep right on going, never say stop.
There will be many on the road of life,
To caution you of the dangers you face,
Suggesting you turn back, and give up the
goal,
And with them your footsteps retrace,.
Right then is the time to show your courage,
And decide for once and for all,
That your life's task lies directly ahead,
And on this decision, rise or fall.
Then in faith push on to heights sublime,
Not back to the land of ease,
You'll always find light, facing the sun,
And shadows in the rear if you please.
The higher you climb, the greater the zeal,
More courage will be given if you ask;
Only be sure you're guided by truth, and
He'll supply strength for the task.

Author Unknown

Youth Is a State of Mind

YOUTH is not entirely a time of life—it is a state of mind. It is not wholly a matter of ripe cheeks, red lips or supple knees. It is a temper of the will, a quality of the imagination, a vigor of the emotions, a freshness of the deep springs of life. It means a temperamental predominance of courage over timidity, of an appetite for adventure over love of ease.

"NOBODY grows old by merely living a number of years. People grow old only by deserting their ideals."

"YEARS may wrinkle the skin, but to give up interest wrinkles the soul. Worry, doubt, self-distrust, fear and despair— these are the long, long years that bow the head and turn the growing spirit back to dust."

"WHATEVER your years, there is in every beings heart the love of wonder, the undaunted challenge of events, the unfailing child-like appetite for what's next, and the joy and the name of life. You are as young as your faith, as old as your doubt; as young as your self-confidence, as old as your fear; as young as your hope, as old as your despair. In the central place of every heart there is a recording chamber; so long as it receives messages of beauty, hope, cheer and courage, so long as you are young."

"WHEN the wires are all down and your heart is covered with the snows of pessimism and the ice of cynicism, then, and then only are you grown old."

This poem was a favorite of General Douglas McArthur and he quoted from it frequently. Attributed to Samuel Ullman, a prominent Alabama civic leader and businessman, it hung on the wall of the General's office in Tokyo.

.................Keepin' On

Keep On

If the day looks kinder gloomy
and your chances kinder slim,
and the situation's puzzlin',
and the prospect awful grim,
and perplexities keep a-pressin'
till all hope is nearly gone—
just bristle up and grit your teeth
and keep on keepin' on.

Fumin' never wins a fight,
and frettin' never pays:
There ain't no good in broodin' in
those pessimistic ways;
smile just kinder cheerfully
when hope is nearly gone,
and bristle up and grit your teeth
and keep on keepin'' on.

There ain't no use in growlin'
and grumblin' all the time,
when music's ringin' everywhere,
and everything's in rhyme:
Just keep on smilin cheerfully
If hope Is nearly gone,
and bristle up and grit your teeth
and keep on keepin' on.

Author Unknown

Indispensable

Sometime, when you're feeling important,
Sometime when your ego's in bloom;
Sometime, when you take it for granted,
You're the best qualified in the room.

Sometime when you feel that your going
Would leave an unfillable hole;
Just follow this simple instruction,
And see how it humbles your soul.

Take a bucket and fill it with water,
Put your hand In It, up to the wrist;

Pull it out, and the hole that's remaining,
Is a measure of how you'll be missed.

You may splash all you please when you enter,
You can stir up the water galore;
But stop, and you'll find in a minute,
That it looks quite the same as before.

The moral in this quaint example,
Is do just the best you can;
Be proud of yourself, but remember,
There's no indispensable man.

Author Unknown

Always Believe in Your Unlimited Potential

Believe in yourself.
You have the ability to attain
whatever you seek;
Within you is every potential
you can imagine.
Always aim higher
than you believe you can reach.
So often, you'll discover
that when your talents
are set free by your imagination,
you can achieve any goal.
If people offer you their help
and wisdom as you go through life,
accept it gratefully.
You can learn much from those
who have gone before you.
But never be afraid
or hesitant to step off the accepted path
and strike off on your own,
if your heart tells you it's right.
Always believe you will
ultimately succeed at whatever you do.
Regard failure as a
perfect opportunity to show yourself
how strong you truly are.
Believe in persistence, discipline,
and always believe in yourself.
You are meant to be
whatever you dream of becoming.

Edmund O'Neill

The Man In The Glass

When you get what you want
In your struggle for self
And the world makes you king for a day,
Just go to the mirror and look at yourself
And see what that man has to say.

For it isn't your father or mother or wife,
Whose judgment upon you must pass,
The fellow whose verdict
counts most in your life
Is the one staring back from the glass.

You may be like Jack Homer
and chisel a plum
And think you're a wonderful guy,
But the man in the glass says you're
only a bum
If you can't look him straight in the eye.

"He's the fellow to please-
never mind all the rest
For he's with you clear to the end,
And you've passed your most dangerous,
difficult test.
If the man in the glass is your friend.

You may fool the whole world
down the pathway of years
And get pats on the back as you pass,
But your final reward
will be heartaches and tears
If you've cheated the man in the glass.

Author Unknown

JESUS

HE EMPOWERED WOMEN

Unfortunately, women are not equally represented in leadership and managerial organizations around the world, especially in churches and other companies that depend so much on their financial, spiritual, and physical contributions. Too many organizations still fail to recognize the energy and talents of women. Some still actively discourage and actually forbid women from taking leadership roles.

Jesus apparently felt differently. His first appearance after his death was to a woman, whose mission it was to go and convince the more doubtful males. One man who was so skeptical he had to plunge his fingers in Jesus' wounds before he would believe. God spoke first to a young Mary about a magnificent plan, which she was able to keep secret until the appropriate time. So, in the beginning and at the end of the gospel, God conceived and helped deliver the message; wealthy women economically supported Jesus and his staff while they were on their mission; and Mary Magdalene and Martha were the first to recognize the miracle of the resurrection when it happened. Although Jesus spent hours walking on the road to Emmaus with his male disciples after his resurrection, they did not recognize him. Mary, however, recognized him almost instantly.

Several men have commented to me that they would promote more women if more women would come forward. Well, we are. Women currently own or operate 55 percent of the new businesses starting up. We ultimately control men's wealth because we outlive them. Women's ideals and methods are causing revolutions in countries, in companies, in churches, and in the professions we serve and are starting to lead.

Consider health care, for instance. Women are swelling the ranks of physicians. Currently, nearly 40 percent of all students in medical schools are female. In a recent survey the number one most requested attribute of a general physician was that she be a female. One local health care authority stated that most female physicians in San Diego have a waiting list.

Men who fail to acknowledge and enlist feminine energy often suffer for their arrogance. Pontius Pilate's wife, for example, tried to warn him not to be involved in the trial of Jesus. "I had a dream about him," she said. Pilate ignored her and signed Jesus' death warrant, and his own unenviable place in history.

Senator Paul Danforth's wife tried to warn him about the seriousness of Professor Anita Hill's allegations about Clarence Thomas. Senator Danforth, like the other males, tried to sweep the woman's complaint aside as being insignificant. The fiasco that ensued was caused primarily by men not taking women's concerns seriously.

One comedienne theorized that perhaps the reason the Israelites wandered in the wilderness for forty years was because Moses wouldn't give Mariam the map.

Jesus said to both women and men, "The kingdom is within you." He delegated equal power and authority to anyone who asked. He said in heaven there is neither male nor female, and He came to see that things were done "on earth, as it is in heaven." On the television show Star Trek: The Next Generation, Captain Picard never went into new territory without the intuitive female counselor, Troi, at his side. Often she was sent ahead of everybody else to assess the situation.

So, men, make way for the women. Recruit them, and you will be the wiser. Women, we must claim and own our power. After all, how far can men really go without us? Only one generation.

Jesus empowered women.

by Laurie Beth Jones

The Value of a Relationship

by Max Lucado

Relationships, America's most precious resource. Take our oil, take our weapons, but don't take what holds us together - relationships. A nation's strength is measured by the premium it puts on its own people. When people value people, an impenetrable web is drawn, a web of vitality and security.

A relationship. The delicate fusion of two human beings. The intricate weaving of two lives; two sets of moods, mentalities, and temperments. Two intermingling hearts, both seeking solace and security.

A relationship. It has more power than any nuclear bomb and more potential than any promising seed. Nothing will drive a man to greater courage than a relationship. Nothing will spawn greater devotion than a relationship. Nothing will fire the heart of a patriot or purge the cynicism of a rebel like a relationship.

What matters most in life is not what ladders we climb or what ownings we accumulate. What matters most is a relationship.

What steps are you taking to protect your "possessions"? What measures are you using to ensure that your relationships are strong and healthy? What are you doing to solidify the bridges between you and those in your world?

Do you resolve conflict as soon as possible, or do you "let the sun go down when you are still angry"? Do you verbalize your love everyday? Do you look for chances to forgive? Do you pray daily for those in your life? Do you count the lives of your family members and friends more important than your own?

Our Master knew the value of a relationship. It was through relationships that he changed the world. His movement thrived not on personality or power but on championing the value of a person. He built bridges and crossed them. Touching the leper...uniting the estranged...exalting the prostitute. And what was that he said about loving your neighbor as yourself?

It's a wise man who values people above possessions. Many wealthy men have died paupers because they gave their lives to things and not to people. And many paupers have left this earth in contentment because they loved their neighbors.

My most valuable possession is my buddy.

A Different Way

God,
Help me to begin this day in a different way. Help me to begin by giving thanks, for another chance to make a difference. Not only in my life, but in the heart and soul of someone else. How God? How can I be an instrument of your peace, your love, and your way of life? Today I will not fight against things, or search out what seems to be wrong. I fill myself with what is good, life giving and warm. Today I do it for you God. For once, I live from my heart. And if I do only one good deed or reach one person I need, the day was a total success. For in that one moment, this world was changed, into a kinder, more loving place. What a victory! What a gift! What a blessing! And God, help me to see that in the end, what I will be left with, is what I give back. May I do something for them. May I live a while for you. May I sleep this night in victory!

Author Unknown

Thinking

If you think you are beaten, you are;
If you think you dare not, you don't;
If you like to win but think you can't
It's almost a cinch you won't.

If you think you'll lose, you're lost,
For out in the world we find
Success begins with a fellow's will
It's all in the state of mind.

If you think you are out-classed, you are,
You've got to think high to rise;
You've got to be sure of yourself before
You can ever win a prize.

Life's battles don't always go
To the stronger or the faster man;
But sooner or later the man who wins
Is the man who thinks he can.

Author Unknown

Don't Let Discouragement Control You

An old fable tells how the devil was asked to show all of his weapons. Many people came to see them. Some were familiar– Power, greed, pride, envy, jealousy, lust. He unveiled all of his best weapons attractive to the eye and beguiling to the heart, useful to lure the unwary to destruction of spirit and flesh.

But one weapon in a special container he saved for last. Slowly the devil removed it and said,

"This is my best weapon.
This is discouragement.
It is the wedge I use to try to break the strongest soul. When it is effective, I always win the battle."

Discouragement is always a possibility in our lives, often as a result of stresses and strains of living. When discouragement comes, we are admonished in scripture to turn to prayer, support one another, and believe that God is with us in the struggle. There may be no easy answers.

But with God's presence there is always hope, and no hope can triumph over discouragement. Today's hope can become the seed of tomorrow's victory.

Author Unknown

Your Thought Pattern Will Determine Your Life Pattern

"One will not find the true fiber of a man in times of prosperity or success, but only in his resiliency and attitude through times of failure and adversity"
Dale Brown

Success habits are mental choices that emphasize the power of attitude. You possess the most powerful weapon in the world—that power is your ability to choose your attitude toward all the events of life. Your commitment to success habits will determine the happiness, love, success, and peace that you seek in life because they are built entirely upon the foundation of your own attitude.

Throughout your life you will eventually be faced with discouragement, poor performance, failure, self-doubt, criticism, sickness, injury, heartbreak, and many other burdens of life. The only way to get through these tough times is to cultivate the proper mental attitude and understand that the intended outcome of adversity is to develop a complete dependency on God. The tendency to give up is in all men. and to overcome this monster, God gives us the weapons of hope, faith, and the freedom of omniscient choice. In life we cannot avoid change, we cannot avoid adversity. Freedom and happiness are found in the flexibility and ease with which we move through change.

Once you embrace change, you will manifest your destiny—
Your thought pattern will determine your life pattern.